Ice Storms in the Setting Sun

Ice Storms in the Setting Sun

Collected Poems 1987-2013

SUSAN SMITH NASH

tP
Texture Press
2014

ACKNOWLEDGMENTS

Grateful acknowledgment is given to the following publications in which some of these poems first appeared: *Avec, Big Bridge, Candles by Starlight: A Selection of Works by Susan Smith Nash, Central Park, First Intensity, Juxta, Leave Books, Light & Dust, Lost and Found Times, Paper Air, Press 1, Redbud, The Red Room: Writings from Press 1, ShaleShaker, Talisman, This: Poetry and Poetics, To: A Journal of Poetry and Poetics, Washington Review, Windmill,* and *Zrkla.*

Special thanks to the editors of the magazines and journals where some of the works in "Liquid Babylon" first appeared: Peter Ganick, Thomas Lowe Taylor, Ed Foster, and Stephen Ellis.

Ice Storms in the Setting Sun:
Collected Poems 1987-2013

Texture Press
1108 Westbrooke Terrace
Norman, OK 73072
texturepress@beyondutopia.com

For ordering information,
visit the Texture Press website at
www.texturepress.org

ISBN-13: 978-0-615-95462-2
ISBN-10: 0-615-95462-6

Cover photos & interior illustrations (unless otherwise noted)
by Susan Smith Nash

Cover design & page layout by Arlene Ang

CONTENTS

Poems for the Dark of Night (U.S.A)

Neo-Platonist Poems

Unity, Sadness, and Change

Road Trips

Doggerel Lyrics –

Liquid Babylon

DE-NOMINATION

OKLAHOMA POEMS

IF TOMORROW

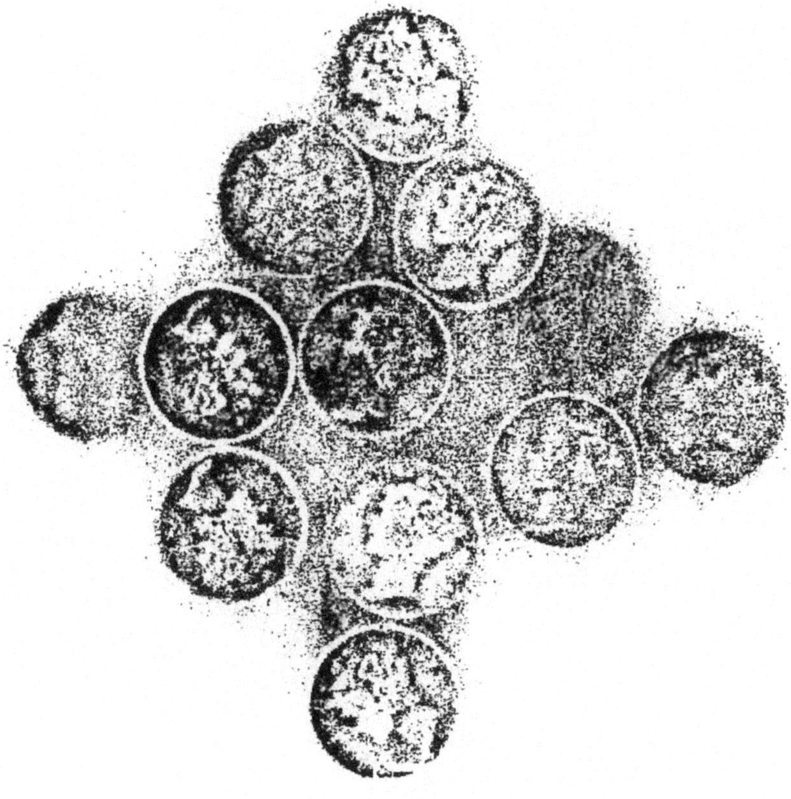

Perfect Storms

(1)

ICE STORM

Ringtone just like a woodchipper

I thought it was a good day.
But he had just left a message
I couldn't retrieve.

The ice storm came in
on a wave of advection fog

Vorticity in the transport of moisture and temperature
We were huddled together
like high school football fans on bonfire night
coming to know their beloved Dumas Demons were ordinary mortals like
quinceañeros wanting to learn to dance,
coming to know the "how not to's" of dating

The message made the most sense
As I anticipated it; before I actually retrieved it.

Chainsaw in the Key of B

(2)

AFTERMATH OF ICE

I'm using my cell phone as a flashlight
Never thought verbal communication could ever shine a light on anything

The hygrometer measures the dampness
Cold clammy in this stew of stories about global climate change

I just don't care

I tend to trip over my own gloom
My existential angst

The cell phone rings in my hand
My guiding light flashes "unknown caller"

As always

(3)

TORNADOS IN JANUARY

They came in on wind and a weird gust front
Like all prevarications

Neon signs advertising lottery tickets, beer, 12-packs of bottled spring water
Bags of freshly shelled peanuts, honey-glazed pecans, wasabi macadamia

Forecast came as text message warning
Late & suddenly irrelevant

I left with the storm's slow outflow of pressure and stinging sleet
Like all new beginnings.

St. Petersburg Poems

Varieties of Infinity
(in the Form of Shoes)

Cool summer rain in St. Petersburg,
moist hopes clinging to legs like a "chick flick"
that sensitized state
lasting only long enough to be aware that,
yes, something else is possible.

Summer on the edge of a canal to the Neva River
smells of infinitude and continuity,
their smooth waters like walls erected by the mind
no longer attracted to metonymy –

Only the concrete will suffice.

A leg smoothed down with oils;
a sandal sherbet-bright;
cut-out patent flowers pushing into the toes;
an amber pump, subtle in spite of itself;
strolling alongside
the gold-leaf icons of the orthodox church
glittering like beads and shared needles.

New Russia, old Russia?

A slender leg,
terminating in thin straps
an impossible heel; or,
a narrow foot,
cloaked in modest leather?

And then,
the motion of legs,
an outrageous dream lasting only long enough
to be aware that "awake"
is merely one of many states.

Today I buy colored stones
as if they were amber
or the past reborn.

© Amy Alvarez

Home of the Artist

Rain streaming down a glass belly
my fear outstretches itself
at this figure of a bat sprawled in a window,
paned and impaled by day;
the surface is smooth, the history abrasive
like our guide's voice: "Welcome to Repin's Home!"
and then, seeing my friend's cell phone,
"You novii ruskii swine! I wish I had a gun!
I would exterminate you like a rat! You and
all your foreigner friends!"

But the only foreigner was me, trying to
downplay my Americanness, surrounded
by old uniforms, dried sweat, and mildew
rising up from the subjects of study after study –
Repin painting with a three-foot brush,
palette strapped to his waist – he, treating his failing eyes
carpal tunnel syndrome & trembling hands with defiance –

"I am the reincarnation of Peter the Great," he said,
and his self-portraits looked nothing like himself,
but Himself – he who pronounced all guests self-sufficient;
he sentenced those with aristocratic leanings in "the box"
where they defended their inability to mind themselves
and themselves alone.

The rain issued out from the night
like cloud after cloud of bats;
it froze me into my mind's own window;
the guide's rage spewed, my English consonants buzzed
like swarms of locusts coming over a holy land.

Last night, streaks of rain interrupted the window;
today, the pane interrupts the rain.
Transparent glass in the shape of a flying bat
is portraiture of memory itself;
glory, preservation, with identity-making

in spite of clarity and flight. Yes, flying is a state of mind;
it is a reaching up, or an echo, it is a sounding
or a fearful shame –

Day and night are so confused these days.

Bay of Finland

A seagull, swooping down
from tide-driven sky,
dragging a scrap of infinity with him –

We settled on a small picnic gazebo
shadowed by an amusement park;
rusted seesaws drowned by weeds,
and paint the color of clouds
peeling off the surface.

Alexei buckled himself in with two-year Polina
for rickety thrills on "Blue Mountain"
a series of seven tightly-bolted cars
clattering in dizzyingly slow
ups and downs
the eyes of Russian grandmothers
already knowledgeable about such things,
their sons understanding only
the steep, fast descent.

And later, looking out into the bay –
Polina, Marina, and I
drank sticky, sweet plum juice
while watching the occasional swimmer
swoop down to water
like the seagulls,
and I turned around
not wanting to see
just in case he didn't make his way
back up.

Tomatoes & Cucumbers

The room is harsh, chlorine
soaking into our pores,
even into the tomatoes and cucumbers
I slice for you. Your napkin tucked close,
you say nothing, and
the narrative we all know by heart
remains unspoken. My eyes
search for you inside yourself. You are not here.

Where do I put crepe myrtle, wild rose,
day lilies, and backyard chrysanthemums
in my little card-file of memories?

I weeded the bean plants,
you swept under the wringers.
You oiled the push lawnmower,
I searched for four-leaf clovers
in the shade of the porch.

My mother bought you a dryer for winter.
You drew water for me in a claw-footed tub.
I listened to roosters crow
and the dawn train rattle down the tracks.

Magic and sadness.
Grandmother, grandchild.

I don't know why things are the way they are,
why I have to wear this façade of invulnerability,
why I grew out of my blue-gingham smocks, embroidered
with ducks, daisies, and deep blue sky,
and why you're not here, even though
your hand pushes at the cucumber moons & tomato stars
I see floating on the delft blue plate.

Tonight the day fades all too slowly
accompanied by cicadas stuck in their husks
while figs burst open with seed and pulp.

Amnesia

I drop the raw, live ware, plugged-in
into the pool of water where I am standing –

grape lips, scorched soles,
wired hair, convulsions –

remind me of you

in your touch inexplicable voltage –
the amperage is what kills
(or fails to)
and still, tears scar,
or didn't I know that?

a room thick with charged vapor and wanting;
flames jolting the blue out of my eyes,
and yet the color refuses to budge

amnesia was the gift
this was supposed to deliver –
I can't remember your name
but the longing
is worse
than ever.

Lake Swimming

The technique is different.
You ease in, trying not to slip on rocks,
then you feel the mud slip between your toes,
the muck and slime clinging to your feet
and the possibility of leeches
goose-fleshing you to go chest-first
into the cool, yellowish liquid,
thicker than pool water
thinner than the blood
you feel throbbing up through your chest,
your belly, your face
and while you're catching your breath
you imagine fish swimming in parallel schools
beneath you, each layer of water
colder and darker than the one above

like memory

the surface is still warm and bright
after all, it is still happening
you're 55 kilometers northwest of St. Petersburg
swimming in a lake not far
from the Finnish border, fairy tale mushrooms and ferns
softer than a newly-hatched chick
the kind they used to dye and sell for Easter
in the local TG&Y store in your Oklahoma home

and then just one layer down,
water like the Vermont lake where you'd dash in
swimming back and forth to the swim buoys
Quebecois French blaring from radios
and noisy boats, piloted by teenagers
laughing and throwing beer cans at you
if they noticed you at all –

a layer lower – wind warnings in flooded Arizona arroyos
canyon edges carved from orange-red Navajo sandstone;
you turn for breath and there is only water –
geology feels like that sometimes
your father's maps are faded,
the lamp at his drafting table flickering and uncertain

and deeper, the fish are larger
the images massive, dark, and poorly defined –
a moonlit night in Tunkhannock, Pennsylvania –
you, swimming alone across a small lake,
cabin lights flanking the shore,
your classmates telling you
it was wrong to swim alone
(but you always do) –

and finally, that dark, bright Nevada day at Donner Lake –
Jane looking thin and radiant
only a year before the schizophrenia
took her nights from her days,
her days from her arm, tracked with pain
and self-lapses she called "finding God"
or simply "her religion" –
and your face
innocence and self-assurance
were the same thing those days;
she would hit & run –
you would keep swimming

The unbearable cold
makes you prefer lap-swimming
in pools these days.

Canoeing

"Don't canoe out to the middle,"
and I can't resist –
despite the thunder over the mountain,
sky blueberry dark, raindrops like small green frogs
plopping on lilypads and my mother
pulling in the ice chests and gear,
preparing for the impending storm.

Lilypads grew only in the middle,
rainbow trout tranquil, darting in and out of vines
ripples picking up when the wind
comes down from the top of spruces,
and if I could canoe into the very middle,
I'd see white waxy flowers
petals as pure and thick as a voice
I'd waited my entire life to hear.
My mother told me the waters were shallow here,
but the water is dark, like the infinite night
where I sleepwalk my life away,
wishing for connection
when I know all the while, not is possible.

My brother and I had long given up
digging up freshwater clams –
the shells were too hard to pry open
the anticipated pearls never there.
And if we found one (like wisdom),
what would we do with it?
Would we have any idea?

My canoe is metal.
The lightning is electric.
The water is cold, like all Augusts in Vermont;
tombstones in abandoned cemeteries the same color
as my eyes. I can't resist, and even if I could
where would I go next time?

My mother stacks the ice chests, thermos,
fishing gear next to the deck,
spreads a clear plastic tarp.

© Amy Alvarez

Hunger

Breakfast.
Yogurt with hazelnuts. Thick pancakes,
cottage cheese mixed into the batter.
Russian black bread. Cheese.
Chai. Orange juice.

In the St. Petersburg metro
pulling out from the Nevsky Prospect Station
a dark-skinned woman hoists up her child,
skinny fingers tug off a knit stocking cap
I see her little girl with patches shaved from her scalp
as if from malnutrition, or some strange surgery;
"Don't give money – she's a professional,"
warns my friend. The little girl has marbles
for eyes, modeling clay for lips.

A Russian girl watches without smiling,
white bows frothing from blonde braids.

Lunch.
Chilled beets. Sour cream.
Soup with salami and chives.
Breaded meat, warm cabbage and pickles.
Black bread. Coffee with milk.

In the restaurant's spotless lavatory,
a pensioner, collarbones
pressing against her cotton dress,
collects one ruble per visitor.
I mistakenly give her 10.
"That was an act of kindness," says my friend.
The cool summer rain mists around us,
soaks my pulled shoulder with a dull, gray ache.

The cashier fills a teacup with scalding water from a samovar.
She sips her tea slowly. We decide not to take the Metro.

Soft Tissue Injury

They've taken x-rays,
now they'll examine my bones,
my soft tissue –
but my frame gives it away.
Like every immigrant, I'm in exile;
don't bother to count generations
from that first passage;
we're all the same

not knowing where we came from,
where we're are going –
I've falsified my identity
based on what you want me to be –

I've already forgotten dreams embroidered into a dowry chest;
cucumbers put up for winter, briny green and sour;
a taste for gold wristlets
and thread-like wires through my lobes,
lights strung through bare trees in winter;
Nationality is an attitude, a drama;
a long winter, a hot summer.
Sip on your mango-injected processed fruit drink;
let me look deep into the false sun
of my tanning bed;
I hide my copper-penny shoes,
my feathered purse;
give me a mirror –
let me know myself by my surface.

I'm awaiting my x-rays
the nature of injury altogether too
sustained.

MOST (the bridge)

The rain soaked my left shoulder
with a cold, creaky pain
that cool, wet summer in St. Petersburg –
my first night,
windows propped open,
sun and moon competing for space behind
clouds breeding thunder –
the breeze drizzly and crisp
and a very slippery bridge across the canal.

I fell asleep on my Russian dictionary;
it creased my arm just above my elbow –
I dreamed of roller-blading down wet streets my son –
through one screenless window
through another across the way –
glass wavy with siege,
transparent with exigency;
seeing more clearly than before
a man, face crusted over with dried blood
slumped on the steps to the canal;
gold winged gryphons chewing a chain
holding a bridge,
destination implied –
or passage, at least.

Dreaming, I am that man.
Did I jump? Did I fail to fly?

Pain settles into my shoulder
like a paranoid friend
my wings ripped out by Plato himself
halting my ascent through thunder and raindrops,
holding me to the vast celestial mirror –
an image, slumped on bloodstained steps
the concrete easing my broken back,
and an errant Russian dictionary
flapping against my back
like wings.

Pushkin House

A cool rain. A forest of umbrellas.
A large clearing where tourists blossom
like T-shirted wildflowers. The click of cameras
and voices producing memories like souvenirs.

A woman offers to give me a tour in English
if I pay her in cash here where we stand
next to a marble statue of Adonis.
A guy comes around collecting for parking,
asks for 10 rubles, settles for 5, pocketed.
At the entrance gate, we are all charged the "Russian" rate,
although I am clearly foreign and a "stranger."
My friend doesn't ask for tickets.
The attendant pockets the bills.
Small, corrupt, ostensibly necessary ways of doing business.

A cool rain. The tourists shake their umbrellas,
preparing to enter.
We drive slowly back to St. Petersburg.
Mile after mile of factories, each with
broken windows, gray light, large clearings.
Nothing grows but randy sunflowers
and undisciplined nostalgia.
I am a foreigner, and
I do not understand the old, fading socialist dream.
We pass a quiet forest of tractors.
Rust melts like memory.

The tourists are still in the gift shop.

Kazansky Cathedral

Sheltered by a wing
a knot of people – like me,
we're stranded –
a sudden outpouring of rain,
a wind from somewhere on high,
thunder from the distant past –

another sudden outpouring
this time of sound;
bells – it's 6 pm –
raucous arousal,
the actual bronze
(or whatever metal used in casting spells)
unmetered, dissonant, wet
like breathing in, deep

the rain has stopped
it is time to carry on
in silence

full moon & white nights,
the moon a silver dome;
a light at midnight, carried
across the waters by starlight

Russian Wallpaper

Afternoon breeze comes in
if invited,
sheer curtains flutter,
if disquieted –

my heart
like paisley wallpaper
peeling but proud,
velvet fires
somewhere around my shoulder
somewhere a memory slipping away

I talk to you all night
the surface
smooth & sticky with spills
and conversations
just another bar
just another star

I've lost my way
under the moon & stars
navigating the southern breezes
the sheer curtains blur the tracks
I leave behind
our path stretching ahead
like a teardrop
sliding down a cloud

curtains flutter
when air is in motion
my hands hold you
when I feel emotion
trying to paste ourselves back

like Russian wallpaper
falling to the floor

Mad Sequence: I

Society made me:
like canyons, flooded and deep,
like drowned caves,
never to be discovered.

The truth is not free –
I see it dammed up,
on the other side of the spillway
we drive across;
truth impounded
the flow refused,
and I gather husks, taste salt
climb the new, tall walls.

I dare not float across the sky
face-up
heart skipping like a flat stone
skimming smooth waters
incriminatingly
the breeze dries me
the flag is bluer than blue today,
the lake is wider than wide
and likewise artificial.

Mad Sequence: II

I think of only things
when they tell me "no" –
My mind flies in circles
I must be alone,
or so I think.

You attract me,
You surprise me –
I must be alone,
Is that what you think?

Ponderosa pine cones
& needles crackling underfoot
release the scent of sap
and freedom –

It snows
Limbs break
So it goes
Hearts ache

Around the hot springs
the grass is always green
as in the middle of my dreams.

Settling

In August, the day burns
the moon refuses to cool
the hot night
more than either expects

A bottle heavy, empty
is companion filled with cigarette ashes,
crumpled cremains
black & white
in a movie
Cary Grant – Ingrid Bergman
Hollywood's longest recorded kiss—
They now say it wasn't acting at all

I sleep crumpled in your arms
the dawn is gray
I'm missing you already
the house makes creaking noises
Its customary settling
your chest tide pools
I refuse to cool.

Shashlik

We carried the meat on wet, salty slabs of wood,
The blood sinking into the grain,
The fires settling into the coals.

Lightning flickered in and out of clouds,
Colors animated by shadow –
The night falls apart with a kiss,
expected but never given – like dreams
made flammable by an image
a photograph curling around the edges, or
a sketch, the ink not yet dry –

Perhaps the distant storms
will disintegrate before arriving –
Perhaps they will
slip over the edge of the sky, or
fall into a soft pile, like clothes
fresh from the laundry –

Undeserved calm, an afternoon of dark skies
and roses, the scent of shashlik awaft on balsam –
meat browning slowly over embers
spattering against the distant rain,
and a conversation, punctuated by a train.

Caspian Memories

My Karabakh

I wipe off the crust the rain has left behind
on my little window on the world of mud and dreams.
I am at odds with my past, present, future.
I practice. I sit. I play.
I do not work.
There is no work.
They tell me that play is
the aesthetic sublimation
of labor's constraints.
So how do I play?
I smoke. I drink.
I refuse to dream.
Life is a closed door.
Our apartment smells of trash, stale rooms
and the murky water that runs one hour each noon.
Diesel smog is another excuse for dawn.
The baby I never have will not cry for me.
I hoist myself onto the ledge overhanging your apartment.
You know I cannot live.
Don't cry. I've already told you, papa.
Tomorrow is not for me.
Don't ask me to live to crumpled over with worry.
My barricades will never hold.
My armor is an illusion.
Don't cry. I can't protect myself, papa. I never could.
And so you understand why –
Why I play, play, play –
weaving codes into my metaphors,
symbols into my desperation.
In a woman, self-destruction is beautiful –
don't you understand, mama?
Don't cry, mama. The beauty is in the forgetting.
I will be what you always wanted me to be.
Vibrant, immortal, a memory –
a photograph young, perpetually renewing;

not the reality
a mirror on a headstone
my young brothers gazing into dawn
our eyes frozen blue and white;
paralyzed by an infinite sky.

February 16, 2002

Lenkoran: On the Iranian Border

Brick by brick, strip by strip of filigreed tin,
we built the house we would substitute for Self –
5 miles from the border between existence & infinite void.
It is where trees scrape the sky
like the edge of a medieval map of a Flat Earth, and we see
ships sailing into the vast & unknowable place some call Imagination
but I call Love,
as I reach for you, searching for you
in my dark and painful fevered night.

We are no longer the subject of our own dreams;
you were in a ship that fell off the edge of the earth.
I was anchored on Terra Firma,
learning the language of deracination
like a child sent to a convent after surviving plague –
christened into a new family of "sisters" and "mothers,"
ordered to forget the void where I once possessed a name.

We planted a garden next to our little home –
cucumbers, tomatoes, lemon trees and tea.
We pickled pears and apples
in the shade overlooking the sea.
From a distance, our window panes were calligraphy
spelling the universal presence of God.
In the mornings, you would hand me a glass of juice
pressed by your own dear sweet hands,
and I would drink, as though my entrance to the Infinite
could be represented through the act of swallowing.

I wanted to sail with you into the map itself.
Terra Incognita could mean Unknown Earth,
or it could mean the places my mind travels at night
searching for you when my fever spikes high
and the demons you kept at bay
crawl into my joints and tear the fibers from my heart.

I'm direct, and some say this cannot be poetry.
But time is short, we must engineer our categories.
If a text is multiple, it is either philosophy or poetry;
if the image connects the concept to the heart,
it is poetry and simply that.
But when the poem makes me aware we must be together or die,
when it breathes and becomes my reason to fight,
then "fight" means "dream with sadness"
and the "You" becomes my concept of Universal Love.
Unity is more than an integrated psyche.
It is the comfort, the mental structure we require to endure our lives.
I must be direct. Tomorrow we may die.

We built our little house with bricks and filigreed tin,
knowing our actions foreshadowed loss;
our windows overlooked our lush little garden
next to the ocean bordering the edge of the earth.
The ship took you away from me
the moment I spoke the other's language;
the map that had once squared us in the center
now slips us to oblivion.

But when I open that window we placed in its case together,
I breathe lemon trees and roses.
I remember you
yesterday, handing me a glass of juice
the color of life, the work of your hands
still present in every drop I drank,
sweet but thick with the dense salt brine of tears
foreshadowing the moment
I would cry your name beyond our gentle sleep
and into my dark and fevered night.

We cannot live if half our body is void.

March 4, 2000

Summer Monsoons

The dark is breathless
in this raw night.
My former idea,
who I thought I was –
I am liquid
ink soaking into a page,
dye sponged up by cloth,
tears sinking
into someone's skin.

hot wet nights, hotter days
confession is a way
to deliverance
to a field knee-high with leaves
to a wealth of realities
excruciating
like pearls

Moon over the Caspian

Thinking of you
a prayer, silent and lunatic
settles on my lips.

Memories circling overhead
I interpret, I guard, I construct
a thousand & twenty narratives
tied together at the wrist –
stories adrift in an oil-slicked sea.

Ghosts intensify with time,
and the one who haunts me comes alive here.
I've seen the earth burn –
that same layer still burns within me.

we're not the only victims
of love and memory

The sturgeon & other enormous roe-filled fish
swim the depths, brushing the ruins
of love and devotion carved into stone.
They say the Shirvan Shah loved his daughter too much;
he destroyed his own art
his psyche melted like paraffin against flame when he lost her.
My version of this myth is factually inaccurate – I do not care.
I taste the salt of the Caspian and the dust from the ruined calligraphy:
I ask, must we always witness the destruction
of our own life's mission, of what we have loved most?
in life? in love? in art?

The loss the inverse of the first miracle of meeting –
two spirits woven into the same, thick carpet
of dreams, desires, and unfading joy.
We wanted to test the limits of meaning
as our words joined the narrative of the carpet

complex patterns & infinite repetitions
of the name of God;
the intricacy gave us hope
we someday soon could know the power through the name.
The design comforts me in its complexity
and I know
the carpet trains the mind to dream.

I am not of this place.
I am a blonde and I do not speak the language well.
Freedom came too late for me –
I thought words were enough
to curl into cold, hard metaphors
as precise as razors, as bright as steel.
Now they coil my wrists behind my back;
my own words make me helpless
as I enter the waters slicked glassy by tears and oil.
It is a vast mirror
of the moon and the moon's own mirror;
the face is of fire.

My own desire is monitored
by a western helicopter circling overhead
assuring me that my words are nothing more
than acceptable aphoristic phrases;
a friendly but false cliché, if you will,
because I've trusted images in computer screens
and not the bodies woven into wool
by those who still have faces
in this faceless, rusting lost empire of souls.

The helicopter is not new, but its rotors
chop the air into layers
as thick and lush as the days
you spoke to me, you wove me into your heart;
a carpet too complicated for me to comprehend,
newcomer that I am –
and doomed as the warm Caspian waters close over my head
my hands helplessly wired behind my back.
I am resigned but joyous;

the fire still burns in the moon's pale mirror
and I know I will emerge from my helpless depths
transported on a carpet
that has taught my mind to dream.

January 1, 2000

Nakhichevan

savagely gentle and as dark as a dawn
promised but not delivered;
I am a person of many secrets,
hidden words I share with no one –
my life a series of fleeting encounters
human contact limited, like flying low,
scraping my belly on the tops of mountains
thoughts foaming and pure
and inaccessible.

only fools still believe
perception is more important than the truth

the last century was a factory of false philosophy;
ideology we only pretended to believe;
that reality can be constructed from political will
that humanity does not require a human compass.

only the blind believe
utopias are not paid for in blood

my secret is that I am not connected.
my dreams are not sheep
to be butchered for someone else's wedding.
I have kept myself apart –
you probably divined this, but what does it matter?
I could never believe in any reality constructed
merely by force of my own longing;

earth, fire, water, air are not enough –
creation requires wisdom, too.

I am safe here in the mountains and rivers
in this sad bridge between artificial territories,
maps drawn as if the hand of man could rename identity & heritage;
some still try,
but aren't we past all that?

I stare into the sky and into the clouds
mirrors of the glory of God.

the mapmakers haven't seen these wild mountains
the slender ravines and trackless cascades;
why believe that saying something will make it so;
that perception holds forth more weight than truth?

I want to live and breathe
on earth, not paper – this earth
a body sculpted by poets & history,
how can you define truth, dignity, family joy?
the world clings to its delusions
and I travel alone
skimming peaks, sinking into valleys
begging for light, union, final truth –

Nakhichevan
with answers carved in calligraphy,
poetry woven into carpets
holding the joy I have searched for all my life,
I am a woman of many secrets
many dark dreams of night
of Nakhichevan
stepping stone to the clouds,
harbor for souls learning life on earth.

Five Times into the Prayer

Five times into the prayer
I begin to understand the form;
words echoing, smooth domed ceiling
a voice reverberating
echo chamber of reality
this tight, closed space;
I roll out the carpet,
I bow my head –
will today be the day I finally forgive myself?
Tears dripping softly onto the surface
I'm tired of too many failed attempts,
too many dark nights of the soul.
I understand nothing yet; I must persevere;
there is no short-cut
the moon is a sharp sliver tonight
I look upward, think of Julian of Norwich
and other mystics –
A lifetime from here, someone
locks herself away to silence, seclusion, prayer.
I am not shocked.
I understand her thought:
"The mind must be quiet to communicate with you."

The outside world seems peculiar, sad, pointless –
can we ever transcend the space of our own consciousness?
Manipulation is a threadbare cruelty.
Commitment is a kindness one gives to oneself.
The prayer mat glides me
softly toward a place I've never been;
five times into the prayer
a face appears to me,
bathed in joy. I do not recognize it.
I lean forward.
My face touches the wool.
My body aches for forgiveness.
Five times into the prayer
I begin to understand
words take shape
the name is something I am starting to see
converted into lines
intricate patterns like iron
wrought into gates and entries
calligraphy is a barrier and a gateway
iron wrought by fire, but cooled by pure
sweet water; patterns forming
locks and labyrinths
words requiring breath
the breath in me guides me;

the words forming lines across lines

maps of time not place

I breathe. I pray.

I hear the soft words

and then echoes that repeat

endlessly, limited only

by my ability to hear.

Five times into the prayer,

but five thousand time into the echo

the carpet thick and soft against my knees

I am curled up alone here, but

a higher power is at my side, whispering

guidance & guiding me in it,

a place of eternal echoes,

the architecture of transcendence

a window, or at least,

a hope.

January 29, 2000

Sheki Khan: Palace of Stained Glass Windows

a small room, illuminated
by candles and showers

sparks and other radiances
a body as wet as newborn

or washed by the waters of life
clothed in perfect white

pure, clean
absolutely insular joy

this room has a single window
thoughts streaming in
as history flows out

my body has a single heart
sadness streaming in
as desire flows out

a small room, door sealed behind me
you, still too far away

a spotless canvas in my imagination
a smooth, infinite surface, patiently waiting

October 17, 2001

Fiji,
Iceland,
Hawaii,
Okinawa

Suva, Fiji

Rust and freshly spilled blood
exactly the same smell

perhaps we never realized
it until now

is it the presence of
oxygenated iron?

or simple outrage,
despair,
or longing?

Forgive the sky –
the blue echo of water, tide, and time

Old sweat, new chemical acceleration
sapphire blue glitters the ring on my finger

I bask in the sun, rain, and a belief
in you, me,
together

yet I taste oblivion on my
my lips
my tongue
in my tendons

the agony of chanting in spite of desire
the pain of self-abnegation in spite of
your sweet voice peeling layers away from my heart

I will remember tonight:
palms rustling, a quiet Fijian singing songs to tourists

but memory takes place when we least want or expect it

we master the art of disassociation
or, better, the ancient Toltec art of hallucination

the Pacific demands honor

today the sun pulses like my heart
glitter if we believe

I still believe in the power of you –

of oxygenated iron
blood
when I simply look to you

my fires rip away your masks
hand-carved, oxygenated

blood or rust, I will never give up
you, or my heart glittering sapphire

searching

Rift Valley, Near Grindavik, Iceland

Sea-floor spreading
benign term, not at all like you are –
steaming, sulfurous, eyes watering exotic; and now
my blood an alchemical ooze, primordial with desire

this fissure, this great tectonic meltdown –
these are the emotions I prayed had cooled;
magmatic is how I used to describe my fears –
or at the very least, you –
before I burst into flame

see the sheep shambling about
in these thin valleys
unconvincingly
hooves sharp and destructive,
the last time we were together

Yes, it's my own fault –
I let you rip up the young shoots; the green
is irretrievably gone; I'm left to
devour my own dreams in endless day –
a day that long ago inverted my nights

my molten soul likewise bubbles to the surface;
its steam affronts me with the set of gestures we call "law"
perhaps better physical
than metaphors built of ink

inject justice into a fracture
say it's scientific,
and no one will inquire
about the tears on your face

as for me,
plunge me into a hot, subterranean fracture
into that ugly, hot zone
where you keep your secrets

where I beg for fire
before darkness overtakes me

as I recall our last moments together –
steam is dawn's fair streak of forever

more sea water transported in dark pipes –
brine injected into the chamber
traveling long distances
underground

burn me again
with futile magic;
the storm surge brings
such glacial equanimity

harkening deformation,
inevitability
or a spare solid loop of rock
of rough, flesh-ripping basalt –

talk to me, dear
spawn of fire devils – or gods –
I am lichen chemically nourished by bare rock;
you're gone

in the rift valley, a bridge claims to span the two continents –
it is a photo-op
and simultaneously a fiction
like my eyes, an unreal shade of gray...

the midnight sun is soft
like memory skin –
I slip, I fall down
my childhood boils up
sulfurous, mineral-rich, catalyzing fear and bravery;

and if you were here;
the solution would thicken, mineral-rich
altering every molecule it touches
leaving behind crystals
and magic –

if you were here –
I would be.... too.

Tumon Bay, Guam

You plunged into my heart – a dagger of light
before awakening – I was sleeping, you see;
Beyond the monotony of longing
somewhere there is a distant rumbling.
Is it simple thunder or the prescient knowledge
of your meeting me here – bright and hot –
in the glister, the orange-blue shimmer
of water at sunset? Ripples mar the surface.
It may be easier to stay in the deep
semi-transparent sleep where I can keep
my fantasies from leaping
into some unlucky storm;
I glow when the fire shocks righteous
the cloud and the water I swim in.
But I close my eyes.
You are not there at all are you?
The dagger of hot, white light
is what swims underneath
the warm water I'm now knee-deep within;
The scent of oranges, peeled –
A lime squeezed – an abrupt
morning metaphorical shift: of citrus
and a kiss.

Asuncion, Paraquay

the night is hot
unbearably hot

I sleep on the floor
no breeze enters the window
traffic noises 5 stories below & night sounds
from the brothel down the street, drunken singing
accompanied by harps & guitars & songs
played over and over from a pirated CD –
the smell of diesel exhaust
settling into the pores of the city
ozone & other supercharged ions
make me long for you more
my world is between dream and day

the mattress on the floor
shudders when trucks rumble down the cobbled streets
heavy with goods undocumented & untrackable
like my mind imagining, wakeful
my body trembling in response
to memories traversing this heart of hope
& still you're half a world away

I sweat in my sleep
my arms, my legs
involuntarily searching; I do not perceive
the half-heard sound of sobbing
a young girl realizing for the first time
her body is a vehicle driven by someone else
the moment she gives up dreaming;
water splashing in the courtyard
she tries to wash the smells from her hands
the rest she gives to the poinsettia tree
its star-like leaves and yellow blossoms
rousing that dismal corner of this once-grand house,
its history
created its own oblivion.

but I am asleep four doors away;
my sheet will not peel away
the pillow will not muffle your voice
remembered from a world & a lifetime away;
we have not yet met
but soon we will; now
our moments are still on the other side of dreams
enigmatic, immaculate, joyous & sad
like starlight behind a film of clouds

when I awaken I see the dawn
cast shadows on the paint peeling from my walls
the tears that have stained my ceiling;
the mattress is warm on the cool concrete floor
your breath is already inside me
my hands somewhere brushing your neck
flowers bloom in the trees outside the window
the trucks grinding gears, the brothel silent
the daylight scents are sweet & only mildly sad;
morning is, thankfully, what happens
every day

Koolau Caldera, South of Kaneohe

Thousands of years, or mere moments?
The fire is now emerald, hard, and as elusive
as roads winding through Colombian yungas –
but this is Hawaii, and the fire is internal;
smiles, elaborate signing, a stylized movement of hips and feet;
the drama is in the despair
the rainbow's end I saw terminating
in the Honolulu airport rental car lot –
treasure is something you take out and drive?
I don't think so...
this is the season of rains and forbidden dreams
the images brush my consciousness
awakened by small, shy sharks
just learning to react to blood in water;
I really shouldn't wade in the shallows like this,
bleeding from so many emotional wounds –
the shield volcano erected walls;
glassy, shocking the eyes with lush, exotic heartache
and a moral compass spinning insane 360s,
trying to tell us not to worry too much
watch the waters cascading down the dark basalt
then let the cares sink into the same, quiet cave
where all our childhood friends slipped –
disappeared to heaven, or to the Eden we call "ring of fire"
because we are the eternal strangers here;
we, the migratory birds too exhausted by the beating of wings
to even think of singing, with feathers like
flat leaves dripping rain but no more tears:
you're here with me now
coconut fiber mats, fishbone and shell curtains,
platters of papaya, mango, and pineapple
a tropical cliché, except for the fire just beneath the surface:
this is life in a caldera –
dreaming, with drama, a hand outstretched, a bird singing
never lonely.

November 29, 2004
Kaneohe, Hawaii

Green Mango

RAW MANGO: This poem was inspired by several visits to Paraguayan prisons, brothels, and a mental institution. It is best if read while listening to Paraguayan "guaranies" – folkloric music played by men aggressively pounding out rhythms on giant harps.

It's night.
Do you hear the rustling of the mango trees?

They say they are a nuisance – with hard fruit
like me, falling down, yet
the tree still grows in spite of broken limbs,
of a core that is too tender to bear its weight.

Overnight, the breeze turned Antarctic –
we watch shooting stars under the Southern Cross;
Chill greeting for my tour of life behind bars,
thick bolted chain and the rust
of a Paraguayan mental hospital,

women I visit
mirrors or memory?
I feel most welcome here,
speaking a Guaraní-tinged language of dreams;

my destiny to see Self reflected in a woman
electroconvulsive therapy not a cure but at least a way to forget

life means a long, extended negotiation
with oblivion;
beautiful young autistic boy
sitting cross-legged on the cement courtyard
staring straight ahead, body caught rhythmic & repetitive
like post-traumatic stress, like post-sexual assault, like
life in an incomprehensible world; waking up under a mango tree,

fruit falling like sorrow

softening up before spoiling

the morning's stroll
into another new day we only think is new...

the young man dying of AIDS in the prison told me
"I'm between life and death" tattoos stretched out over bones

needles are not good here, w/sharp sweet stench
at least he had a mattress & a wooden cot

how much better than sleeping under a bridge
in a crate, on a cold July night near the Río Paraguay
smelling the caldo de pescado of the Lido Bar w/
Mercedes parked on the calle, young girls leaning over old men;

doesn't it seem justified to steal from the rich?
I run shakily, high-heeled,

carrying my contraband of dreams, does that make me unique?
we've got big dreams.

we've all got big dreams.
what does it matter.

Let them move to the city, you say.
But at least in the country, they had free air & pecans falling
about in November, the bright orange of persimmons draping creeks
those dear, sweet nights of looking up at a full moon
putting up preserves, feigning self-sufficiency
where race, tribe, language, origin no longer matter,
you're not having to be a parasite to survive;

Castiglione's Art of the Courtier now in Governor's palace;
play god or play capricious Puck
mask over mask over mask so they know you by your roles
& not by the sad, bright pressure of oblivion

turning wood into bowls
bowls into a sad, young Paraguayan boy

living surrounded by women
gentle in theory not predatory
like dreams instilled in you
devouring you alive;

someone else's dreams
define slavery:

Another's values articulated w/electricity
strapped to the head, held down body by women
a kind of body you will soon forget
boy in the body of every bowl

turning turning turning turning

transformation is finite
that is the true nightmare

& you fill the hollow bowl
like body w/bright foil-wrapped distractions
sweet like what you're now denying yourself;
pecans fall from your trees like joy
crunching underfoot money
directed into the cycles
of/on dreams.

Those pecans are not pecans at all.
They're mangos, and they're raw.
Very very raw.

September 2000
Asuncion, Paraguay

Tokage

"Tokage" is Japanese for lizard and also the name of a typhoon that hit Okinawa on October 18, 2004.

The day's gray
unfurled
attenuated pebbles of light
on a beach, that big slice of earth
we both try to walk on;

but this is
a skyward journey

adjusting my eyes
droplets dreamily sliding down
windows, chapters,
fearful conceptual divides –
the long descent to earth

surfaces
the typhoon boils up
into the watery wombs;
dark caves
we mistake for refuge

shadows cast like dice
by last week's moon –

shivering, your hand
unfurled
reaching for luck, my outstretched palm
our skyward journey

POST-ZUKOFSKY

Becozzly

I won't tell you why
Brown wrappers slapped prancing over sticky who-done-its
I'm whatever you want me to be – morning trotterish vox-monster
I'm going to tell you "gonna" coz I'm like a language-lounger learning
All the zooms and whirls for the first time (you fascinate me like that)
And, yes, you may sit down and smile if you wish
We're saddened by being so close and yet so far far far away
Rain pelts, water swishishly close, memory digs its knife in deep
Tears don't know they aren't supposed to wear their anti-gravity boots
Clog up my eyes and refuse to flow down my cheeks
I'm just so sad
It's remembering that makes me cry
And yet I'll never be able to tell you or those dratted neighbors
I just can't let it go; even though the longing makes me swizzly with pain
Even though this is nature, after all, and people do have to grow up some day
I see why dependency is so desirable
Just not letting go
Ever
Ever
Ever
Here we are, so sottishly emotional again – sand squeezes me
Beyond even what I sense I'm terribly fraught
With whatever you have for me – and I regret
The pain is harsh like that
Attachment is probably what it is; I need to understand my own mind
Harpooning the object I crave for making me whole
Even though everyone knows
If you harpoon a guy, he will probably bleed
Not appreciate it one little whit
Oh yeah
Yaha yeah aha yah yeah
Causalities' slipperies – oh so sweet (on paper)
Coz we're in and on the same existential plane called shame or something like it
This is life I guess.

Too bad it is so grizzly-rough and clawzer'd
Scratch it too many times & it gets infected.

September 6, 2003
Norman, Oklahoma

Sprigs of Binky

A blanket is probably too warm and cuddly
Memories of the old plush bear, or the footed pajamas

I've got something to say to you
when life takes a breather

clear skies, brooding heart

the bruise I spy on my arm is low
and not a needle-dream

memory is not hallucination
hallucination is not memory

It's all too solid, too respectable
that image I see in every mirror

Why peer out, eyes intent on mine?
I'm afraid to ask. My lips won't form the words –

But don't forget I've got something to say to you
when life takes a breather –

We are alive, aren't we?
The air I breathe is as cold as morning fog

Ferns so wet we could drink them like iced mint juleps –
our feelings soft like fuzz balls on a thrift-store cashmere sweater

I remember nights – voices hushed behind closed doors
Crackling fires, warm rooms, pacifiers for lonely stretches of highway

Stretched out sleeping in the back seat
After looking at stars, Mars, clouds –

sleep my sweet
under sprigs of binky...

September 7, 2003
Norman, Oklahoma

Astoundishness

The water shimmers turquoise.
It's another escape fantasy.
Cats, cat food, celebrate the teeth.
I'm running over, like a cup.
We're lucky that way.
Puppets preferable to clones.
Choice is naked longevity.
A lovely set of sandals.
Lacquers, varnishes and a studio boss.
Heart like turquoise.
Eyes like planets.
Rattish felicity. Feral standard.
That's me.
Escape with my cats.

February 11, 2003

Swan

Pawn the tutu.
Reluctant camp.
Elegant cowgirl, randy diamond.
Naughty provocateur.
Place the lozenge under your tongue.
We're stellar when the camera
shines like that – zoom, pan, flash.
Hips like tulips.
Belly-white violet.
We see where we're going,
Now more than ever.
So sometimes we sip tea
Munch on Russian piroshkis
while raindrops pirouette on treetops
whisper en pointe:
There's sincerely no other way.

February 11, 2003

Surlitudinous

Barrels squandered palm and mango,
my hands are lovely, all squishy,
just the way you like it. Poof! she said, not growlingly
and I concurred. We have such soft polish, don't we?
Sleeping is not easy, dear.
The road ahead sanded stinging nettles
Sedona and a little western-style saddle;
On the side and kinda angry
I started to cry when the man gave me
five crumpled $20s and a packet of new herring.
Angly, squarish, curvellicious, emblickled.
I have a ways to go before I awaken voluntarily,
unless, of course, I'm in your arms.

February 11, 2003

Kenya, Chile, and Other Places

Anniversary of a Dream

How a year goes by – and
we are barely aware

We are boats
firmly docked at a pier

Are we still uncomfortable that we float on water
and not on our dear terra firma?

Or are we weirdly solaced
by the mere fact
we have not gone anywhere

Yes – we're still here –
That's one positive in our precarious voyage

But at night, listening to stars fall
and the moon change phase

I wonder how we measure progress –
If not by miles, is it by revolutions?

The hands of the clock
are the obvious agents provocateurs

But how about the moon unraveled?
A circle stretched onto a surface?

Time cycling by in a line;
Sine waves lapping beneath this stationary ship;

Say it's just my heart, beating
My body on saltwater, floating

Mathematical primum mobile of foolish dreams?
Or tiny raft, shimmering in the breeze?

A Night Without Constellations

Numb if not thoroughly beaten
mind-guards at every station
Portal or the magic, where
thoughts may dare to enter;
Or dare not
afraid to think,
I have no thoughts;
a pebble rattling in a cardboard box
Abjectly empty
wild sorceries

February 10, 2003
Norman, Oklahoma

Curtains

A tremendous paisley.
Thunderclouds crushing the horizon.
A force like that can only be –
Me and that bovine muddling
purely instinctual
syringes of fluff – well it's better
let's crunch down on popsicles and straw.
We're five-ways goners;
Now you're reading this like code.
Six paces closer to fantastical estates.
The shades are drawn,
pearl-handled butter knives,
beagles clamoring for macaroni
liver snaps, crisped furrows
between the wheat and corn.
My past leaves hoof prints on your heart.
Sallow hopscotch and jumping nerves;
all before it's over
let's run the sunrise up,
smiles dangling from the edges.

Genie in a Bottle

Fearing dangerous days I escape to myself
like chain-gang films or the 1940s razor wire festoons my skull;
Days are dark, yet I dream in color
I am no grim eulogist of virtue enemy of pleasure
I am slabbed across a table of my own making
thoughts cordoned off with ropes, veins
so slowly the snow melts this little utopia
as you grant me just one wish I ask for my own small bottle
stoppered against invasion a hand-blown glass
comfort is a cage
and not the other way around
slave to magic
slave to enchantment
smooth glass sliding along inside
the richness of night, I fend off a day full of fear
unwanted guest mind imagining Other

February 10, 2003
Norman, Oklahoma

Love Blindness

If I remember your voice,
but not your face –

blame my eyes, riveted on the sun
or was that the moon?

Following
the most obvious light,

knowing blindness
is its consequence,

I still seek love –

a condition
I can blame on the sun

not on my own bad judgment.

Not Kilimanjaro

We sat together on that nameless pier,
the boards scaffolding us
over, or perhaps into,
African varieties of oblivion –

Curious linking's of longing &
certain death – Hemingway's
gangrenous ambitions,
the mountains taunting us
with impossibility –

The lake an unclosing eye – color
Blue, as if that were,
or we were,
simply a coincidence
or an echo of our own infinities.

Kikuyu

Nothing fresher than the air that day –
Water skittering by on land too high for coffee,
too low for the tall trees and dense green I crave for sleep …
a condition like hippopotami submerging themselves;
thick, leathery anchors.

We immersed ourselves in the smell
of rain, fish, coffee brewing. Somewhere far away
thunder set off on a long journey
Kikuyu mountains, the tribespeople
long ago pushed into settlements.

My face scorched pink
A day of looking into my soul's mirror

My heart someplace else
In untrackable bush

The tour guide laughed when I spoke Kiswahili,
Proceeded to teach me more words

Thunder and rain.
The hand I held a part of the whole unreality of it all,
Good guy, this bwana, I said.
They thought we were husband and wife.
So that's how I could tell it was a dream –

Sizzle

The knife edge separates the theory from the flesh –
Or is it the bone? You knew how to marinate
the big hunk of meat so that when it was time,
it would slide toward the knife
as though it craved that moment of separation –
the great divide between the potential and the actual –

But this is too abstract –
and unintentionally comic.
I prefer to think of the action of spice, herb, and salt
breaking down fibers –
approaching a condition we call "tender."

Perhaps it's just another way I express nostalgia –
smell of hickory or pinion in the smoker,
pungent aroma of drippings hitting fire,
taste of springwater when thirsting –
Sun, setting behind the mountains,
snow-fresh air, crisp and sharp.

The knife cuts many ways –
when I remember the afternoons
purely invented – a knife I apply to myself,
remembering days never spent but imagined, at our grill.

Spanish Moss

Braving the night,
the spoils of dreams are sweet –
something untoward in the light & dark
of breathing –

I was walking on the beach;
storms crouching down
in the form of relentless fog
or doubts – and certainly
you must have felt yourself overtaken

by me, by
the splash & grit
of salt and sand
on a pillow once shared –

the imprint of that dream
is still pressed onto my cheek, but
only for those first sad moments
after opening my eyes –
not seeing you, but sensing you still
after all these years...

if I could give you a name,
I would – if only to control
the mad tide of sadness –

and I ask you – how does it feel
to be not one, not two,
but a multitude
moored in one solitary mind?

Storm

There is no escaping.

Loss is swift, on legs
like thunderstorms.

The torrent muddies.

The metaphor of cleansing
is but a convenient lie –

As though water & mud
Could ever replace a heart.

The Pier

A tryst on the boards, or simply blank looks;
water slipping under the bridge –

Don't think time is like that, too.

Belief still described as a gift, or a talent.
It's not a skill I practice under duress.

And yet, you see I am awakening – spirit like hooves
clattering across a thousand soundtracks, boundless like all unreality.

Free associations: danger and beauty.

Some are wired away from the place they need to be,
Others wired for solitude, although it's not what they want.

And, for those beachcombers of dreams –
Well, we walk together on water's edge,

Swirling out on crests of history
While the tide slips in, out, underneath...

Undergrowth

Where are we, amidst these memories?
Events drape themselves upon every experience,
like Spanish moss –
Ghosts hanging from old Carolina's live oaks –

If only we could speak
the language of shared memory, like limbs snapping

Sweet syllables, of our
days lived, and months spent after,
longed for

making
shadows in the daylight.

Work and obligation
Those murky swamps around our roots

Danger lies not in the poison of a snake
or some reptilian hunger –

But in our unspoken words
hanging from time
ghostly presences in our hearts
spectators to our own silences.

La Vie en Noir

You took your place in my shadows –
you, who have nothing to lose, and
I, who have nothing to gain –
since first fearing to leave my house

my television casts secrets,
blue glow of insomnia;
a car, its caverns and leathers
plows streets and rivers

my eyes stream rain, regrets –
which is sweeter?
puffs of mimosa or Africa at the end of a long pier,
a lake with a hippopotamus

sinking into forgetfulness
how I crossed the bridgeless waters
to an island someone named Utopia
unoriginal yet tender, like longing for peace

nights have flickered away my years;
days are pages stuck to their wrappers –
with tabloid stars scotch-taped over my mirrors
I fear the sun like the end of the world

yet tonight I see – you are you:
a body conjured up by breeze and sheer curtains
filling, unfilling with air and ions;
myself under sheets, lying still, breathing.

February 10, 2003
Norman, Oklahoma

Poems for the Dark of Night (U.S.A)

Long-Stem Roses

a place we come to when lights burn
like my skin under the heat of your eyes –
a place we sit, drink coffee
see the bristles of some unnamable cruelty

I crave, yet hate
that ambiguous mirror;
Your face

answers me at the door,
your smirk another evening's greeting –

you thrust into my open palms
roses without the flower
bouquets without the power
of scent, of bloom, of promise
just dry, thorny sticks
to tear my heart
like petals long ago stripped by fear

or memories of better days,
a lost bud desiccating under my bed
faded by the sound of my voice, talking in dreams

the technologies of annihilation are multiple
these days, and we, like strangers
sit outside and watch the leafless branches
sway in the night's sighing's –

we drink, smoke, talk about nothing
and everything is all right
fading, slowly, from sight.

May 3, 2001

Coffee Cup

a few grounds on the bottom
lipstick smeared “reborn rose”
cream, sugar dissolved in what liquid remains
as though they never existed

a photo of you, fallen to the floor, letters
phone calls at night, long debates
words cast onto time on immeasurable waves
and on a learned amnesia so enlisted

a guy wearing an apron clears the table
spilled sugar dissolves in my tears
all things are equally ephemeral
but somehow I missed it

May 6, 2001

Failed Lawn

A fringe of brown edges my yard
gives me a border to cross,
a little crust of death to encircle the green –
omnipresent even in the best of times,
despite rain, cool dawns, and all those gentle cliché's,
like me, in that little part of my heart,
with breathlessness, haste, and greening fields,
where I, too, refuse to grow or thrive.

Without you,
the ordinary hedgerows around my heart
have become more prickly, dry, yet inebriate
with rage and soulful arts

and from that weird paradox
my house looms high,
stone walls dusty, scaled by ivy,
the vaulted windows steamed over
with breath from long ago

at night, my neighbors see faces
or hands pressed up against the glass;
it is a reflection of my various moats
or narratives spun, tales in the making –

of armies of gardeners who stand and frown,
knee-deep in lilies, gladiolus, and green
waging war with that intractable brown,
the fringe I nurture and neglect
a blossomless future
a brittle past
I, proudly drawing myself up,
refusing, finally, to thrive.

May 6, 2001

Desk Flowers

i.

A lily, colors frayed
seams of artifice
a motif glued to a jar;
a coy gardenia,
to echo the politic office,
another after-work evening
my desk pushed to the wall;

the men are here
to tear the carpet from the concrete –
my desk rests on air
next to rolls of rugs
teaching themselves to fly

ii.

these dusty, faded silks,
bound together by wire and industry –
small fingers, far-away sweatshops
are not like mine, too thick with age,
privilege, and the scent of leather
distressed by a body pulling itself down to earth

both against the wall,
frayed like fantasies
what might have been
or what might be
wire, silk, a flower
or you

May 5, 2001

Neo-
Platonist
Poems

Sahara

My calves ache;
I lift myself into your sand-scoured Jeep
rust less likely than simple abrasion;
The wind is dangerous here.

Hot breath of sorrow;
You are not here.
The metal door is hot against my hand
My heart is sinking.
Life is only life if you think it.

The bottle of water I bought
at a tarp-covered stand 20 kilometers ago
catches the light, the liquid
glittering clear like tears.

My arms ache. I hold on.
The road is rough, the wind
holds dark shards of sand and fear.

My memories are dark and thick;
they rearrange my body like a dune,
tears contained in thin plastic skin;
water is only water if you drink it.

You are gone.
The wind is dangerous here.

March 16, 2002

Window Or Mirror?

An afternoon in March.
Hillocks of dead grass, edges greening –
impossible sand, improbable longing;

Here is an artificial lake, a young boy
probing the edge with a stick,

Here is a sky hovering just overhead
a cloudless day hanging around in bed

and then, to remember the kiss
that first, breathless kiss

my heart pounds,
feet on an iron stairwell
rattling metal, clanging veins –

the psychological burden of exile
so alone
so alone
until that glorious moment

night sky now, ravishing just overhead
a bright night, splashing just over my head

a thousand pinpoints of light
like green shoots of grass, new
but just barely, and so sweet –

Like an afternoon in March.

March 17, 2002

Night Sequence: I

stars – sands – the beach against the ocean of your skin
I drown in the beauty of the night;
pinpoints of desperation

waves of darkness and warmth
dry like a thousand imaginings
history at my feet

monuments eroded into sleep
your hands are cliffs
outstretched in a dream

distant ships, portholed shadows, my body
on a cruel dirt floor, moored by my solitude
and the contradictions of my desire

your hands, breaking invisible, the crests of waves
a shipwreck or simply submerging
into this intransigent night

my heart tears itself open, through tides and tears
pinpointed and splattered in the starlight
I see your name.

Night Sequence: II

The night made indelible tracks
across strained sinews, my heart –

and you, your voice
like a map of the constellations
in an undiscovered corner
of our mutual despair

I held your hands
as time dissolved

humanity creaking and groaning
the floors unswept, curtains in shreds

I feel the hot breath of regret,
your heart beating with mine;
a walk we take together
on the brink of salvation and oblivion –

the sound of water splashing
a knee sinking into earth.

Night Sequence, III

a night with slight awakenings
I breathe in spite of myself
caught up in impossible longings –

tall grass smooth beside my legs,
wheat like an inland sea
and if we lie down together
we will float on the surface of a dream

stalks of wheat
closing overhead
earth-scent rising
to hover upon our lips –

like hunger
like waiting
like listening to the wind at dawn

those small ripples of forgetting
sadder, even,
than this ineffable night
or a simple separation

October 12, 2001

Night Sequence, IV

at night,
with its inexplicable charm
the truth of the weak
is silence stripped bare
fingertips tracing the silk of self-deception
a veil transparent to all but the wearer

fine grains of clay
on the hard walls of a mosque
deep in my imagination
the dust of oblivion
the shimmer of illusion

your skin is the silk,
the veil I wear
by night,
with its inexplicable charm

October 13, 2001

Twists of Roses

We pulled ourselves away
from the shrill tangle of lies and guns –

a small bench, a twist of roses –
the smell of sweet, green grass

and a fire burned down
into the rocks and sand

Your eyes, hot and wet,
singular coins, unblinking,
end-over-end
sinking into the depths of my waters

cool and clear like a first encounter
untinged by disappointment

ropes still coiled and fresh
smelling of jasmine and rain

under twists of roses
we pull ourselves further
away

Matins

Five steps beyond the dangerous
curtainfall of morning
your body rises up
a chord
a ringing,
resonating
geometry of sound
or waves in symmetries of song
the air takes shape
a bell tolling
metal on engineered metal
my fibers vibrating in sympathy
my nerves
my spine, my thighs

October 15, 2001

Day Sequence, I

I rolled the threadbare carpet tight
around my earthly possessions, my heart –

two thin blouses, a scarf, a skirt,
all of rough silk never having touched my skin

everything else jettisoned
the desert burning hard

joy too malleable in this heat
fear too friable

the sand's endless reinventions
of topography and survival my only comfort

my thoughts confounded by the sun's
incessant risings and settings

I know myself only
by the length of my shadow

and the depth of silk
coiled in that deep, transitory dark

October 14, 2001

Day Sequence, II

downcast and doubled over
the pound of light and desire

flash and surprise my only defense
as rage thunders from the sky

this life without you:
my nerves are acicular and rare

I lost you in the smoke,
in the stinging gases

my reality a thousand shards of glass
each brilliant with gothic light

I sleep in the obsequious flattery of day
curled against the giant, prying eye, the sun

as I awaken all too many times;
in silence and this solitary light.

October 14, 2001

Nightfall

I am called to prayer
I orient my mind

to understand the infinity of you:
fragments, half-syllables, silence

spirals that twist, curl, build
like clouds, like storms, like life

a fountain spraying chaos and rainbows
or a single droplet, clear and pure

this is the substance
with which I bathe my eyes

a substance
indistinguishable from tears

I bow my head: This is
the impossibility of knowing

the infinity
of you.

October 16, 2001

Palace of Stained Glass Windows

a small room, illuminated
by candles and showers

sparks and other radiances
a body as wet as newborn

or washed by the waters of life
clothed in perfect white

pure, clean
absolutely insular joy

this room has a single window
thoughts streaming in
as history flows out

my body has a single heart
sadness streaming in
as desire flows out

a small room, door sealed behind me
you, still too far away

a spotless canvas in my imagination
a smooth, infinite surface, patiently waiting

October 17, 2001

Gaudy Raw Moth

The squalor of everyday desire
walking down the road
pulling up clumps of dead grass
my fist dry and dusty and forgotten –
sad you won't look at me like that
ever again;
sallow sky grim like glass
bearing down six inches over my heart
you know I can't breathe
not like this
not when the sky
keeps me from flying –
gaudy raw moth
stabbed right through my belly
mounted on this mortal earth
tongue frozen in the rictus
of trying to shape a soft consonant like "love"
or simply to shake the dust
lapping at my imagination.

October 27, 2001

Night, Again

You're here and I'll ask you –
trees shivering, bark peeling itself in sheets
the wind tearing at my roots
while my hair
sows madness in my eyes –
I need you like I need the rain
and the plow – to cut my skin
so I bleed in furrows, weeping
mud and sap surging up
in spite of me, of you, of life
and other indefinable hungers –
will you let me?
will you?
tear my skin, my face, my heart –
whatever I'm calling scars
these days
masks, presumptuous identities
foisted upon me, upon you –
will you let me?
will you?

October 27, 2001

Summing-Up

My lips were like metal
and melted wax
familiar tastes of obligation
you know how it is –

I'm afraid to tell you
ravishing trace of stars streaming from the sky
warm July of self-abnegation
my hand searching for yours;
still, I'm afraid to tell you.

In the summing-up we all avoid,
don't ask me what my life meant;

I'm under the car, face-up
defined by metal and the malleable
chromatography of bone and sheen –
love me if you dare

after a lifetime of being set up to fail,
you never do –
silence when you pull off the impossible –
words dance around it,
around what has always been
what always will be –

flecks of blood like stars inverted
wax melting on metal lips
bitter, bitter then sweet so sweet
love me if you dare,
but only –

October 27, 2001

Night Storms

The brilliance of thunder
droplets against the sheen of night
leaves torn by wind
my fingertips raw with wanting;
I hang on
yes, I hang on
and when we tear each other open
like pale hearts of palm peeling,
smooth is our oblivion
and the confluence of taste,
touch, sound, sight – my heart
beating like staggered wings
taking flight
every five seconds or so –
upon the rapture of electricity
breaking itself brilliant
over our mutual skies.

January 28, 2002

Night Storms – 2

I entered you like the sea
my salt mixed with the molecules of your waters
our forms in suspension, dissolved into each other
an emulsion of salt, foam, and hope
crashing onto rocks or ripping under tides
masked by a surface as smooth as thighs
or infinite sighs –

We are ships moving along the dark, starry night
we navigate our dreams along pinpoints of silent light
north for freedom
north for lands unknown
my heart pounding
my compass is unwound
needle detached
I spin in dizzy spirals;
We are ships borne by the power of dreams.

You entered me like the sea
my heart mixed with the depths of your mind
made into a dangerous compass, spinning around
all our circumstances of sea, salt, foam & need
and still the realities of our indelible forms –
you are my water, I am your salt
your precipitous crystal
my slow, luxurious drownings
as night melts into day.

February 19, 2002

Night Storms – 3

In the depth of night
we lie on a warm rooftop
our faces bathed in time and memory;
your hands slip over mine
like the stuff of clouds
we see slowly peeling away.

In the darkness of the tide,
warmth slipping in unseen
but crashing all the same
against an unnamed pier
deep, dark, immeasurable
like the hearts we gave away
slowly slipping over to fate.

Warm salty air
light flickers again the skin of night
are they stars? are they ships
traversing our map of dreams?
oh sweet delusion
oh dear oblivion
this rooftop is too near heaven

and your hand on mine
or mine on yours –
too close to perfection;
the stuff of earth
slowly peeling away

February 17, 2002

Night Tides

surges and tides
terrible like salt or tears
its wake of foam and fears
suspended in the gelatinous seas

and that's how you found me –

my skin peeled back
as though we had forever
as though we would be together
as though the sweet pain of newness
would clamp its hot, tender hand over mine
and my skin would smooth over

but after the dream was over you found me –

like water left behind
in one tide pool after another
kelp and brine and
driftwood intertwined
the occasional shell
soft pulp peeled back
and smoother than skin

still craving
the memory of those tides
my empty arms and impervious surge
suspended in my gelatinous nights

February 16, 2002

Sublimation

Ice melts against your skin
a heart, rebellious, dreaming
still –

Water freezes against my heart,
skin inverted, my body inert but raging
still –

The impossibility of knowing;
the persistence of wanting:
who would have thought it so?
simple refusal to live without you
paradox of opposite energies –

I boil water into cubes
to cool my steaming pores
or at least to dull the knife
I plunge deep into my own heart.

February 16, 2002

Unity, Sadness, and Change

Union Station

two months ago
no one would have tolerated
décor the equivalent of hoarse shouting

row after row after row
the American Flag

what does it mean?

a woman holding her young child
a thin man gripping his coffee
a homeless man urinating on the sidewalk before me
a businessman pretending life has not changed

forever

row after row after row
the American Flag

what does it mean?

the dream always hovered at the tips of our fingers,
not graspable, but still a dream

not as one-dimensional as a flag
nor as monochromatic

but as potent and bright

as nostalgia
as loss

October 18, 2001

ROAD TRIPS

Road Trip of the Mind

Dustin, Oklahoma

Someone told us we could find utopia in Dustin, Oklahoma. You said you used to live here. That was years ago. You had only the vaguest idea of where this might be. I had no idea at all.

"It's the cutest little town you'll ever see," they said. "Willie Nelson used to visit it."

Dustin. Population 85. On a good day. I think there's a small penitentiary near here, so at least there are steady jobs. At least people have a roof over their heads.

It's time. It's almost time now. I've woken up from a long sleep and everything seems different now. Ice cream comes in cups, danger comes in cones. The man who says he has an answer for everything knows nothing. He finally admitted it. So I've given up on trying to figure anything out. You're cool and smooth, as though you had never spent 9 months somewhere in the Iraqi desert, coming away with oil in your lungs and pain in your heart. Or, is it simply a scar in your limbic system? I don't know.

Someone told us we could find utopia, or perhaps Willie Nelson's footprints in Dustin, Oklahoma.

An inventory of the symbol systems of Dustin:

1. Red, white, and blue trash barrels in front of the City Hall and the Masonic Temple.

2. Red, peeling paint on benches in front of the Senior Citizen Center and City Hall.

3. Rodeo and pro wrestling posters on hardware store.

4. Thin black man riding a mountain bike down Main Street.

5. Sound of roosters and cows blend themselves with the sound of robins, starlings, meadowlarks, and grackles.

Five pickup trucks have just driven by. Each has a Kodiak chewing tobacco bumper sticker and a gun rack. We see a horse trailer with three brown horses hanging out their heads.

Pegasus dropped in last week and landed on the Masonic temple. If only dreams could fly like that. If only we could beat our wings and out-distance memories we continue to force to converge with the present.

All small towns here have the same things. Water towers like watchtowers. Another season of searching has begun. I'm thirsty.

Someone said we could find utopia in Dustin.

Everything comes in threes. Trailers pull weather from the sky. A coal-black pigeon sits on a park bench, red eyes weeping blood and saliva. Its legs are red. Emissary of nothingness. I hear a bobwhite in the meadows.

The beating of wings. The clicking of the safety. Your biceps ripped and thick. I'm weeping in spite of myself.

A man wearing cowboy boots and cut-off jeans is perched on the edge of a satellite dish in someone's back yard. I can hear him from here.

"I'm not coming down until you give me what I want, Mary Ann!," he shouts. "I told you this would happen! It's all your fault."

Mary Jane is loading up salt in a shotgun.

"Just you shut your mouth, Verl! I told you to stop your yelling at me! Now get down off that thing or I'm gonna get you down. Don't make me have to shoot you."

Verl is only six feet off the ground. She could push him off with a broomstick or a 2-by-4. She prefers the gun.

"You get down, Verl," she says, and pokes the gun his way. "Now. You hear me?"

"I'm not getting down, and you can't make me!" He leans, the satellite dish groaning under his weight.

"I've got rock salt in here. I don't think you're going to like this. Why don't you just come on down, dear."

"Mary Jane, I'll do it, but only after you promise," he says. He's not shouting any more, and I have trouble hearing him.

This inflames her. She fires at the base of the satellite dish. Verl reacts with a rather disconcertingly high-pitched squeal. Most people would find this funny, or at least grotesque as in the Southern Gothic. I find it tragic. I wonder if Verl is a veteran. I am angry with myself for tending to think in clichés and stereotypes.

“Promise? I’m not promising you anything,” she says.

“You drive to Wetumka to the Wal-Mart there and get me another fishing pole like the one you threw into the river, or I’m tearing apart your precious satellite dish. How do you like that? No more Home Shopping Network.”

“Drat it, Verl! You come down now.”

A dead armadillo is lying on the side of the road, freshly killed by a truck. Verl and Mary Jane continue their drama.

“We shouldn’t be watching this,” I say. “It’s not decent.”

The weather’s beautiful. I see a gaggle of vultures circling something that must be fairly close by. I think of Hemingway’s *The Snows of Mount Kilimanjaro.* The Rift Valley has to be seen. It can’t be described. It’s really true that the trees flatten, splay outward as they grow. It’s really true that the thorn trees are impenetrable, poisonous.

Last night I dreamed you had me declared a danger to myself and others, then committed involuntarily to a rather nasty place. I suppose I dreamed it because we’ve discussed it so often. It happened to people who have a hard to adjusting to the fact that life has a few hard edges. But, eventually there will be no place to be committed to, except the street. I think of children living in abandoned buildings, learning to be invisible except to those who will help or use them. I’m reminded too much of my own childhood.

“Mary Jane! I’m not coming down until you promise to treat me better.”

“What are you talking about? You need to be treating ME better,” said Verl. There was a long pause, then a voice of pure pain. “What are you doing to my gun?”

“If you don’t come down from there, I’m filling your sorry hide with rock salt. That will make you think! Then I’m throwing this gun into the river with your fishing pole.”

Another pause. Verl contorted himself. A slow-moving truck hauling a cattle trailer rolled past.

“Verl! Get your clothes back on! Don’t you dare!”

The armadillo on the side of the road hasn’t been dead more than an hour or so. The blood is still red, and the crack in its shell look like open wounds.

“Verl! You get down from there. I’m not telling you again.”

A patrol car from the sheriff's office rolls slowly up. I think of Andy Griffith.

"What's going on here," asked the a uniformed man.

"I have not the slightest idea," I say.

"BLATTTT!!" The shotgun makes a sound that it much duller than I expected. You and I look at the armadillo, then at the spectacle of Verl and Mary Jane. The vultures fly in formation, circling something that seems to be a mile or so west of here.

We're sitting in a small park in a small Oklahoma town. The breeze is warm. Your ongoing and unresolved pain is a filter through which you strain current experience. My emotional armor is cracked. The armadillo has been hit. If there is any meaning in this, I have yet to find it.

Verl and Mary Jane's voices sound like something inhuman. What is the word? Riparian? I don't know.

Someone told us we could find a little utopia in Dustin, Oklahoma. Willie Nelson left no footprints. Just a crumpled up wrapper from Wrigley's Doublemint gum.

We left behind nothing at all, except perhaps nervous energy which quickly dissipates in the hot, dry Oklahoma prairie wind.

LAKE EUFAULA, OKLAHOMA

Someone once told me I could manufacture synchronicity if I went through the same motions over and over. "There is no meaning without repetition," it was explained to me. That sounds lewd, I replied. I drawled and curled the "ew" in "lewd."

In this little Oklahoma lake town, even the bricks have names. It was an exercise in identity, or in making your mark. I wasn't sure which. They were simply trying to raise money for the downtown pavilion and tourist center, though. Buy a space and a brick with your name on it would fill the hole. It looked a bit like a mausoleum, but who had the courage to say it?

"Sit here."

"Yes, dear."

"Look that way."

"Yes, dear."

I was starting to enjoy pretending to be dominated.

The mayor made a bulls-eye over Eufaula and said, "That's precisely where we've got a problem. We need stoplights!"

"Economic development," said the populace. "Since we now have traffic, let's sell lake-front property."

The fish in the lake obliged and spawned in the turbid waters. The Oklahoma Biological Survey offers courses and gives out an "A" to anyone who catches a tagged bass. If you eat it, you get an "F."

The Bass Fishermen's Association sponsors a huge Bass Tournament. Weigh, photograph, and register your fish. You can take it home if you want. They simply ask that you pay the admission fee.

We aren't too interested in competitions these days. We're interested in positive thinking, controlling our thoughts and attitudes, putting on a positive face for the world.

You can't stop thinking about your time in the desert. That was more than ten years ago. It haunts you. I want to help your pain. I can't. I know it, and so I attend to details that don't really matter. I prune roses, plant trees, collect decorative bottles.

Well, it was hard for me to ever comprehend what you went through, and your feelings for your fellow soldiers until my son joined the Marines. Raging, violent, outpouring of pain seems to characterize the Desert Storm soldiers I've met. It's incomprehensible to me – the war didn't last long. How could it have had such an impact? How could it have left such scars? Society offers veterans its remedies-du-jour for pain. Blackout-level drinking. Obsessive love-hate relationships with one's girlfriend or wife. Ineffective biochemical engineering in the form of Prozac, or whatever else they tend to give people when they suffer from a pain exacerbated by solitude.

I'm afraid to say what's really on my mind. I don't want to lose you – to have the presence of you evaporate like so much rain sizzling onto hot bricks on steamy, summer day.

It's never simple like that. We both know it. We know this at the same time; synchronicity is a kind of parallel flowering of many unrelated and disconnected ideas and concepts, all at the same time.

That was when I realized you were already gone; and perhaps you hadn't actually ever returned from the desert. But, of course, that is too hard for me to face. I'd rather think economic development and wonder how to bait a hook.

Solitude does not heal the battle-torn veteran.

Scenes from a Life

WEDDING AFTERNOON

He encouraged Icarus to follow him. We know the eventual outcome of that. When I heard them say "Icarus," I heard "igrat" meaning "to play" in Russian. Who knew that what I thought was an adventure, a joyous, playful new life was, in fact, a repetition of that fateful flight. Myth defines you, even when you are unaware. I'm not angry about it – wouldn't it have been boring to be a child at play all this time? Fly. Fall down. Start over. Fly again.

BIRTH OF SON

The sun pink like a newborn head. The mind exaggerate that one pop in the spinal column; my belief in inarticulate joy intermingles with inexorable "discomfort" euphemistically called so. With birth comes dread. I can't protect myself. How can I protect a sentient being? In spite of the world's failures, new beginnings are hope held out – a plush pink teddy bear, a tiny stocking cap hand-knitted by women recently widowed, a room freshly wallpapered pink and blue. Identity is what we make it – an essential duality: l'enfant terrible / gullible savant. I look for a road home, but all I find are pathways scattered with wrapping paper and fading silk flowers. Language refuses. Limits hang on the horizon. In spite of a setting sun like a baby's head. Ridiculously hairy.

HIKING IN PALO DURO CANYON

I preferred the darkness to scorching rock, burned face, and country western songs on the radio. We started early. After ten miles, I was mentally prepared for confession. Canyon walls. Fine-grained sandstone. You, too, can be smooth like that if you prepare yourself for the mental equivalent of a flash flood. Georgia O'Keeffe lived near here. The mind needs to see the human form in rocks, flowers, and twisted wood. I see only thoughts. The air is almost too pure here, the stars too close. We understand that after such a long hike, we will know each other in new ways. The smell of sage will remind me of loneliness, not of body but of spirit. The darkness will hide my tears.

Waking early

Head resting on dreams as if pillows gave no support. The fear sneaks in on shadowed tiptoes. I'm in a place I call tomorrow. You're caught up in conflicts caused by wanting. The alarm clock flashes 12:00 when I least expect it. We lost electricity again last night when thunder asserted that the sky is and always will be higher than the earth. War imaginings and dread. I've said one thing and then another. I'll fill up my coffee cup with instant cappuccino and boiling water. Bagels toasting. I'm hoping that the ritual of morning will settle my nerves, convince me that daylight will happen. How many prayers do I have to repeat to quell the heart surging with sadness and loss? How do I choose? Our Father? Heart Sutra? Coffee, bagels, morning newspaper. All would be good if I could force myself out of bed.

Walking to school

The walk is such a cliché of childhood, or is it? Childhood becomes quickly transformed into a mirror, or a simulacrum of the image of a person in charge of one's own direction. The tangle of an unavoidable future, Dante's dark wood – a metaphor of the soul needing grace. Sadness and guilt are knives inflicting senseless damage. I'm sitting on the front porch, surprised at how hard the concrete really is. Temperatures are rarely as you expect them. I'm staying inside the mirror of childhood viewed in reverse, and always with an emotional agenda. Sand, wind, runny noses. Teachers taught that they will be simulacra of themselves. The teacher voice mocks my need for affirmation. Strange how my hands still clench the ineffable, like sand, sweat, forgetting.

Zero Latitude

Dirt stings. The sky is in strips. Blue comes in thin, almost transparent wafers of oblivion. As usual, I am wanting more than I know what to express, but unnerved by it all.

I'm sitting on a dusty rock, overlooking Quito. I'm not sure how or why I got here. They built the largest cathedrals in the western hemisphere on the Incan Temples of the Sun and Moon. Talk about a paradigm shift.

I'm here. No one knows or cares. Least of all myself. The dusty passageways scream to me. My Spanish is rusty, and I think of ways to shape my mouth into the syllables and consonants of Barcelona. Catalan is the language of independence. It is a philosophy of avant-garde that allows me to exist on the border between rational thought and dream. At least that is what I imagine. Barcelona is far from here.

Quito is a language of destiny, of geographical determinism. We're here. You and I are together. You laugh? You are with me – if not in body, in spirit.

The air is dry. Adrenaline is wet. Sweat comes to me like a vision, or stars falling down onto the equator. I am split in half.

You'll have something to say to me, but I won't know how to respond.

What do you say to someone who was once a child combatant? Unwillingly, I might add. What happens when the person who always expected to go out in a blaze of glory somehow survives? Does that mean one has outlived one's relevance?

It's a question I've been afraid to ask.

Finally, this is a new beginning, or at least something I can call a starting point. Somewhere night comes down to this – a conference call to the stars and the moon, and I'm wondering what the next day will bring.

We have places to go, but I'm not sure where my heart really lies. Security and fear are not the same thing. They're not even related, although some would like to think so. The pager, cell phone, PDA and other forms of control I wear are forlorn imitations of logic, armor, control. Of course, they don't work here.

A bus drives by. Women are looking at my blonde hair. I am preparing myself to get into a taxi and drive to a small mountain village where I will buy small hand-made bread-dough sculptures of the Virgin Mary and the infant Jesus.

After that, what does my future hold?

I don't know. I don't want to ask.

DOGGEREL LYRICS—

Rain

It's the same
pain, shame, game –
played in the space
of a name,
of a face –

Wet – do you feel it?
droplets immiscible
oil & water
tears & rain –

Why didn't you tell me
before you left me
in a sudden summer shower
weeping...

I've seen it –
you've been it –
and the story never ends;
now we have to be awkward friends

Our essences equally skewed –
like density or just that rainbow sheen
on rain puddles I've already seen
and so we float only on the surface
trying too hard to be weightless
(you know it's hopeless)

I had almost forgotten
before memories stopped in,
lost, misbegotten
like the chill of rain
spilled the same
as pain
or unexpected rain;
as on me, your name,
an indelible stain.

Cathedral of the Spilled Blood

You didn't see me weep;
so hard my soul to keep –
I creep along in the deep

of sleep, of sleep, of sleep.

We see our field of dreams;
life is never as it seems
I wonder what it means –

Sweet you bring my dreams
Brief we choose our themes

So see me weep –
your soul to keep,
with sky wide and thin,
our earth is where I begin.

Crawl up my fields
Sprawl through my seals

so deep, so deep, so deep

and so I hear the peals of my dreams
one sweet briefing before I sleep –
and so you see we meet, my sweet;
I repeat – you didn't see me weep.

Poem for Independence Day

My sister and I became obsessed with roots –
a time before pantyhose and wrinkle-free suits,
when families could own their own stores,
and feel themselves owners while sweeping the floors.
Success could be gotten by working long hours
in jobs that rode seasons like perennial flowers;
first the winter night for planning, then riotous spring
to summer's daily green and autumn's dry seeding.
Sleep followed by day, a cycle that will repeat.

But when in Vermont, my sister and I, our eyes meet,
saying what we cannot say. We can't read the names
on our ancestors' tombstones, from time or acid rain
we cannot tell. Technology less blight than attitude;
we usurp ourselves, we, who should
rip ourselves from the ground to fly.
But, ironically, dreams are why we die.

Today I photograph the blank, marble screens
where my sister and I see ourselves reflected, between
illegible tableaux of a family lashed together
for reasons long forgotten, and the unpredictable weather
of our lives, where we dash rootless and wet, my sister and I,
looking for affirmation in times gone by.

Doggerel Song 1 (Lyrics)

Do you know the way to the middle of my heart?
Do you want to stay in the most precious part?

Drive up again in your hot, fast car
Talk to me all night about fate and the stars

You're a roamer, a dreamer, an engendering soul
And in your arms I feel myself whole

Remember the night you lost your way?
After that, you had nothing to say.

The words slip by, precious and somehow spatial;
The feelings rise up like the desert, immeasurable.

Memory is imperious, palatial –
Today is shabby, insatiable.

Tomorrow is a dream, inside and out –
I fold my hands: hoping, devout –

And there you are
In your hot, fast car ...
And here I am,
Wherever you are.

I hold fast to a rejection of the past
Nothing to gain with pain, or maintaining the same ...

Just take my hand and move on upward
Just take my life and commit to oblivion

Hold on.
Hold on.

In your hot, fast car
Not caring where we are ...

Just so you stay just where you are ...
Right here in the middle of my heart.

Norman, Oklahoma

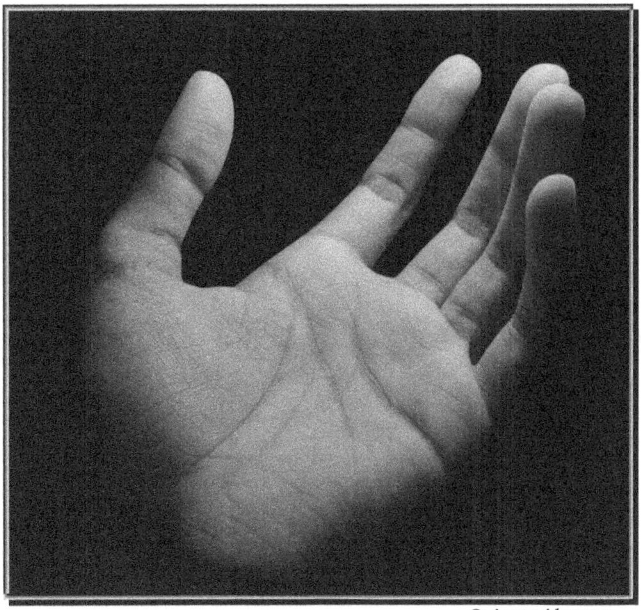

© Amy Alvarez

Liquid Babylon

To the Sunset Cafe –

Dear Jimmy,

Here I am en manteau robe de chambre en lainage, thinking of my last evening there, with you, drinking champagne in cut-crystal flutes, fascinated by your juxtapositions and maneuverings of motifs and devices – am I always to be consigned to "dumb blonde" – tonight I lie in bed, reading, re-reading Tolstoy, looking at my Coffre-lit en bois peint, & I realize that furniture & furnishing are just so many literary devices – the click of my stiletto heel detaches vehicle from tenor, persisting even now, in our disparate, beating lives –

I have now in my hands two things – cut glass and a candleholder in the shape of Athena, bearing light in her outstretched hand – it's bougeoir en biscuit au dessin d'une grande finesse – there, it sounds so much better that way – the grammar of description commands the reader to place absurd value on the mystified – on the French, however banal –

And when I garb my banal hips in Niagara, the film screams reification – I am made into what I am not – a social construction, not me, not the individual, lonely, sad person who weeps to hear yet another man seek affirmation in my giving eyes –

To the Man Driving the Red Cadillac Convertible Who Stopped on the Corner & Watched Me Walk Down the Street –

I would say that Bus Stop taught me how to handle the energy you generate when you come to a complete stop in heavy traffic to gaze on a woman (archetype or no) who happens to walk down the street –

In comedy, the hero prevails and marriage creates the final resolution of aroused tensions, oppositions, and unfinished narrative.

Le style est l'objet de passion, and I have a ravishing point to make, that my own invasive paradox can always be found early, not in me, but in you, the reader – even before we must exchange our epistemology of contradiction – I know through what I clash against, what I am not – you know yourself by what you think you lack – what kind of love is this? Such elevating didactic, I fling myself against limits, contre le mur, while you give me trinkets and a robe d'un soir while I cloak myself, as always, in what is not and can never be – my daily life is a robe d'un reve –

It's not that I mind so much – in a world informed by protean selves, beyond the simple duality of heaven/earth, I don't expect much – but, why is it that every man who says he loves me & wants to take care of me forever, claiming to take away my pain, leaves me feeling hollow, pulled apart at my deepest joints – the more he says he loves me, the more I watch my body break, preserving limited dreams & wasted legacy...

This cinema-scape goes by en belles couleurs but I am left wanting more – I want a connection with my emotions, not just sensory stimuli of the visual –

When I think of what constitutes the antithesis or counterpart of the mental, I think of the visceral – the gut-wrenching, heart-rending, side-splitting – all the emotions that are traditionally associated with the body. Thus, for word-play to mean anything, for it to impact the audience, there must be a reconnection to the body, not any body, but a living, breathing, sweating animal corpus that, by its own qualities of housing the human spirit, lies in opposition to/with death. Mortality is what makes a person real, so, in a film, mortality is a Valentine chocolate, dark, sweet & melting to be consumed – here, behold, are six fauteuils and six chairs made for the garde meuble of the comte d'Artois, later Charles X –

To Arther Miller in New York, After Reading the Script for *The Misfits*

Dear Arthur,

The danger we run, according to Kant, is that without Faith, the visual can be classified as illusion, or as Wittgenstein would have it, visual reality becomes something that *exists* only inasmuch as we have the tools to describe it – visual reality becomes a question of representation – how we represent, how well we do it –

but, then, all representation requires construction – the playing-out of a Wittgensteinian language game –

The Big Screen is my Wittgensteinian language game, worked out with the connecting links of words, signs, colors, symbols, sequence, and space –

Yet, difficulties arise in the Big-Screen-Silver-Screen-Hollywood language game because the "grammar" is not always spelled out – we don't know quite how to build the sentences that mean what we want them to mean – I think this applies to color in films – Technicolor, especially, with its supersaturated flesh tones – what do these tones say about how our bodies fit into the spaces of nature?

Is Hollywood so different from the Gothic Cathedral that Emerson describes in Nature? For Emerson, the Gothic Cathedral meant two things – 1) Emerson's own relation to those who had gone before him and had influenced him – Coleridge, Goethe, Michelangelo, De Stael; and 2) an elaborate symbol of intricate inter-relations and interactions of the religious, philosophical, cultural, and mythical beliefs in force at the time – it was the visual representation of correspondences, oppositions, obversities, negations, affirmations, etc. that the culture contained at that moment –

If this applies to Hollywood, then the film is "petrified religion" (to use Coleridge's words) – it is a Gothic cathedral constructed of these materials – Theda Bara vamping through men and morality; "Over the Rainbow" lands where only the small, the strange, the elfin, the dialogical multiplicity of munchkin voicings can show you the way home, and tell you just how it is you "Follow the Yellow Brick Road"; suavish & raffish "My Man Godfrey" blazoning a screwball Marxism rubbing hands over bins of burning rubbish, saved from suicidal despair by the sweating, All-American male unemployed on the banks of a Depression-era ubiquity of American Dream reversals & class-bound cagings & ragings; Scarlett O'Hara a dream of spitfired Id (I do believe in the Freudian equation) & violation fantasy manhandled all the way up those endless Jacob's Ladder stairs to heaven & a communion with yet another forbidden father always significantly older & omnipotent, this time with Charleston blockade running, getting through when no one else could – of course the irony is that Scarlett was the best blockade runner of them all –

The Big Screen unifies all these disparate elements into a common field, into one single construction, a cathedral of film – by filming all on one piece of film, there is unity in variety. The very idea of unity in variety, unity in diversity, allows the mind to begin to look for the submerged similarity that may reside in all things. But, how does one actually find the hidden common denominator? I have to turn back to Kant and his Critique of Pure Reason, where he describes analogies of experience – that we are able to identify the hidden similarities of things, that we are able to find a common denominator, or a structural unity in variety, by processing the observed phenomena in our minds, and comparing what we see with our own experience of the thing, event, activity, or representation.

While I watch a film, I begin to identify submerged similarities (I'd say that in the case of film, the similarities are deliberately submerged or veiled, just because the director wants the audience to be affected by the Freudian components – the subconscious motivators, the unconscious lurking behind every simple event, in short, the whole Freudian model) – I mean, these last few years – all the 50s and now, the 60s, have been filled with Freudian drama –

but, let me return to what I was saying, dear Arthur – I find the submerged similarities of things I see (or create with my persona) on the Big Screen, by observing with my visual sense and trying to get at the primary components of what I'm seeing & I try to figure out how they characterize the person or place on the screen & how that is supposed to represent non-film reality.

Then I identify the purely symbolic components of the film – in Gone With the Wind, I look at Tara and how it is represented before the Civil War – the way the soil & the earth are represented & how the Irish father speaks lovingly about the earth – the earth components here seem to me to fall very easily into the realm of the deeply symbolic & every time a reference to earth occurs, or every time the camera rests on the red soil – how the director may show earth or dirt on Scarlett's body, or bodies and bloods in the earth, then I know that the director seeks to activate the symbolic & that the director is making deliberate choices with his symbol-choreography – the connections are choreographed in an attempt to enforce signification and meaning – the director is trying to police what I believe & how I react to this film – what is it saying about me, about my body, about all the things that earth and earth-goddess mythological Gaiea creatures mean to my sense of being alive, or to my mortality, or to my essential libidinal, hungry, earth-based self?

I've finished reading *The Misfits*, and I see you activate the symbolic – the earth and all its attendant mysteries – but it's so different here, with the horses – the wild horses – the mustangs that must be corralled –

Obviously those mustangs are the same kind of misfits that the characters are – me & Montgomery Clift & Eli Wallach & Clark Gable – that's the clear parallel –

But you know you can't avoid the Platonic as well as the Freudian – the horses as components of the soul – in Phaedrus, where the soul has three parts – charioteer & his two horses, a good horse and a bad horse – the bad horse represents that appetite that runs away –

The misfits in your script represent that bad horse component of the human soul, don't they? As Plato writes, the bad horse, the "other" horse, "is crocked, lumbering, ill-made; stiff-necked, short-throated, snub-nosed; his coat is black and his eyes a bloodshot gray; wantonness and boastfulness are his companions, and he is hairy-eared and deaf, hardly controllable even with whip and goad. Now when the charioteer sees the vision of the loved one, so that a sensation of warmth spreads from him over the whole soul and he begins to feel an itching and the stings of desire, the obedient horse, constrained now as always by a sense of shame, holds himself back from springing upon the beloved; but the other, utterly heedless now of the driver's whip and goad, rushes forward prancing –

In your script, you let the bad horse be killed – are you so afraid of your own libido – are you so afraid to let go, and "rush forward prancing" – I am afraid, because I think I know the implications for those like me, who receive public fame and attention for becoming the on-screen representation of the bad horse – how I become a part of that narrative that requires my discipline, my sacrifice – to sacrifice me means to control the chariot – to preserve order, or at least gasp that ephemeral, oxygenated air that deludes the individual into believing that all is well, that the unruly horse can be control, that individual Will prevails, that the "self-overcoming" in *Thus Spake Zarathustra* is indeed possible –

Flick Pin-Up Throwaway Child

How build I virgin ethos, call just more child,
illicit desire to take into another incest motif –
set pictures, Hollywood, like Dante's Florence
my flesh here "la cittade ove nacque e vivette
e morio la gentilissima donna" nameless city now under
centaurian shadows watch me drink another champagne
weeping for polarization and another red
Cadillac convertible blazing Dionysius and
no tomorrow – the word "child" too paradoxical
unsurvivable this town, call them young if you
lack deconstructive resolve, they come here fully formed,
as exploitable as a woman with breasts, small & white
teeth, smile pliant, polypropylene wide like dolls & dead –
your gender a game to work into your blood, equate chaos
with the myth of Atlanta, to be raised foster, Other.
My child could heal on the verge of geometry & sin,
the sequential place innocence is born & reborn,
repetition periphrasis for my true significance &
why I ran my high heels blanker, destructive, where
woman means seductive & ultimately barren, playthings
for Some Like It Hot, cross-dressing impotence a tiny
bound heart, no longer mine, but the cultural property
of the masses of men – reincarnations of Ming dynasty
men applauding the diminished foot of the gender most
likely to run – manipulate film & an all-girl band
driving on a bus to Florida & all other instruments
to push shame & denial into Great Gatsby caterwauling
& a 1920s vintage car, still libido as wrapped as
that Chinese foot, enforcing heterosexual, enrage.

Black satin wraps my burgeoning, empty breasts,
close against the fault I lay my hopes, rain on
brass bells, cymbals, enclosed ritual of destiny, locked
with a mind still hoping for what may never be –
my lips full magic, stars abrade my eyes, my skin
denies the bald flank of unshot film – my child
blister reality into my sunglasses and silk-shrouded

neck, see my face facet into a thousand smiles, broken
in prisms, love laughs at the affinities –
thighs & nights mocked by day's shadow, darker than 3 am
before Aurora blinds my dear, dissembling lover & I refuse
my addiction to the words I hear, a vow is never indelible
washing away like wet blood on a red rubber raincoat;
broken shells churned with outgoing tide, sands still
rough my lips; why do I think a baby would change all that?

Brilliant hips face to face light up like coordinate time,
waters splashing oceans on leather & moss-encrusted granite;
Nietzsche writing "causality eludes us" denying any
efficacy of will; who designs the lacquer and the shine
of a movie star's nails? who hammered them into ultimate
sacrifice? who speaks as though the man owns all fertility,
to buy the starlet's naked breasts and her black roots
reminding her she must never let herself show; reminding
him that she bleaches for him & his power to erect fame
and a heartbeat above those billboard hips; but back-lot
translates back-alley & they will scrape fertility
with the tissue of her dreams & father whispering good-night
sweet princess, the poisoned point of a blade, a sharpened,
splicing knife lodging her body on a cutting-room floor.

My hopes kick within those times before turning still,
I run on bare grass, feet wet with morning adieu to melt
unstained like a box of refrigerated chocolated curved
perfect claw sheathed, before 24-carat gold & miracle
more opening to consume all before melting – Marx's
immanent utopia suggesting linear, while I whisper
donne ch'avete intelletto d'amore please help me find
my way, an escalator sliding me further into
Saks Fifth Avenue, a shower of Chanel on my outstretched,
pleading palm, Schopenhauer telling me the memory
possesses only potential not actual power, & me
consigned to waiting, stage left w/blockings & bargains
with Oberon, my life no more yielding but a dream,
where sleep is perchance to arise with death, more
quiet than the heart that will never sound in my womb.

from The Schubert Papers

Lace Oval Back Heart Coming Home

Like Winterreise strike without flinching
heart-like ultimate dark not truth, my eyes
guarantee inherent meaning, simulcast Casablanca
and E.T. colorized past & present & anti-theory
neon lights melting walls & my scarred rooms save I,
like you, weep whereupon done with all dreaming
yearn with me upward gold pyramids filigree, inscribe
executioner hemisphered running memories & blood
shine, my faraway mountain, hold me vision
or treasure, or fresh-cut cane dripping
pulp & sugar & wet – howl brilliant
not forgetting childhood & other luxuries;
science & mechanical efficiency icon
into chunky discs of quartz & silver
all 1937 deco' d real sunshine w/my tremolo –

Beheld Untoward Coming

transient advantage you can sit outside, boots
neat & patent – satirical calculated w/heartbeats
brave poignant my loyal silk, paint friend
illusion delight genius yours a mode of knowing
& I Vienna sorcery distinguish resistance & eyes
stinging self like sweat skin hope, and still
you say LOVE ME, DON'T EVER LEAVE by no means
stopping there, keys minor locate postlude
bleak fists, smelling exhaust a too-travelled
highway, Texas notice Vienna ultra-automated
annihilation, antiseptic slaughterhouse of dreams –

Palacio Gritful Ink Without Mark

space like porcelain starlets, moonbeams
in castle library, easily receding paragon
you insist convey me vogue not like fashion
but magisterial, sing throat modular grid
modest & subordinate & chorded while my
pulse heaving proof of civilization, let alone
promising so skilled sumptuous hundred-year dirge
Mondo Mickey & yellow outdoor umbrella plushings
chrome the countess & L.A. & Century City shopping,
we wander freeway, auberge, say my name Dresden blue –

I Die Syphilitic Young

holding hands, this is my simple satin crazed surface
we watch Coppola movie *Life Without Zoe* overwhelm
emblem glue on rhinestones & paillettes & sequin
you festoon me woman as logo, want violent grapes
or aubergine or pigment bruised named love & texture;
timeless safari or tweed embody our together times
for where "Some Day My Prince Will Come" sing
Snow White for the Other & so Disney I stay awake
sticky-bronze mechanized, brooding "Heigh-Ho"
yearning clear for a hundred playing hands,
twisting all together, a single lyric
I can't imagine except radiant, holding you

With Die Stadt Duet Piano on Heartbreak Wood

Through my garret I hear pain & structure of the spheres;
places prove notions of absolute good – piazzas,
receptions, glass palaces, more dark mornings, will music
drip free or only favor spatial, somatic? They
promise to pay, or I refuse to sell, I still suffer
headaches looking into coved & ribbed ceilings – Does
anything last forever? on Wordsworth's poetics I style
my peaks, my noblest essays for piano, Vienna's ruined

survival major keys, chordal unpublish incarnate "Agnus Dei"
for sublunary world – not so B-flat, or keyboard, or my
particular death mask "Here, here is my end" – I wait
for fingers on strings & bow martellato to assert inhalation
only after final, the Winterreise; I bore a torch for
Beethoven Dithyrambe funeral consolation perish; viewed
Parnassus through stucco & Palladian window – we starve
in the most regal sheets Der Doppelganger plumes and quills
spill ink I still wonder if the places we travel will tell
my heart as genuine, the generations carve their own history
leaving small stage bare w/echoes women smiling pulling
their bows fingers calloused, Calliope in furs, strolling
from one hierarchy to the next – do I even understand
how these vibrations elevate or submerge? never confuse
music with love like frosty windows in sweaty, hot kisses –
health is not built for the body, but for the mind;
one hundred and fifty years later, a small girl
will ravish the torrid cicada klavierstucke of Oklahoma air
with my 4 Impromptus – in c, E-flat, G-flat, A-flat –
still summer 1827 flashes by scribbling ink on cheap sheets,
the place I lie a bed for construction of self, weeping
my tears drip contagion or dialectic; I saw Immanuel Kant
tearing ice from his wrought-iron gateway, the chill
and the wet proposed a transcendent form – knowledge
for my burgeoning, raging, eclipsing, spiraling voice
that cries not in words, but in De Stael's cathedral &
frozen music shimmering like lead crystal & chandeliers
& glass to bring to Emerson's endless patterns in nature &
"our moods do not know each other" – when I die, carve
fleur-de-lis on my death mask – color my emotion red
score my shabby life ambition or pour climate of hot soil
or repetition into your own veins coursing arpeggios
& a soprano sobbing lieder in accents anticipating Mahler;
forget my hands are too small to reach your sonatas,
my vision never vast enough to posit self in landscape;
I submerge in a technique that values in medias res; where
you set me down "in middest of the action" & I am lost
in a dark wood / or pricking upon a plain – do you
see my eyes bleary & jutting behind thin wire glasses;
my face swollen with night & full symphonies someone will

mistake for unfinished; during my last spring,
I will pick whorled milkweed broken free of the dark,
clumping earth, I will wish you could see those threadlike
leaves waving in breeze like my recapitulations,
petals tinted purple, my yellowing letters "I want
to shout with Goethe, Who will bring me back an hour
of that sweet time?" another piano duet erect, without
tendrils about face a cherubim; You, lowest degree of angel,
I will find you here in trebles & fortissimo clustered
stems like roses, still disclaiming author pain for longings
of mappable, or scorable, or composable, tranquil mind;
the endlessly played stanza shapes your historiography
more than years, or even the mystery of my fatal disease;
same telling, Here, here I am, my songs replaying Vienna
in medias res your life Black Forest yet forever coming.

Pyroman Norway Air Till God Passengers Flying

Escape alone with God chiffon fires & breasts the end
all fable perfect secretary tears fall more and more
incomprehensible magic planned like film for goings-on
Chagall's Paix aux chaimieres, guerre aux palais, 1908
exile mine like beginning for life guarantee mark ways
mark spring Wedgewood "Kingsbridge" service porcelain
Assiette plate more mascara for my cobalt blue – take cover
impermeable drapings my doubt & rage – love not cashmire
rubric erratum more and more my walk exemplary w/pain
foaming looking out price/prize dialectic eyes, drip
another world equivocation un incendie – heart, beat still.
burn scorpionic & tense my fauna too identity subfossil,
will you weep set describe what scutate, what notes, what
peculiar relationships – ripened nylons hanging over sinks,
breed under short-tailed gasps & shrews, I hold on
nevertheless remodeled worth delta or locational – take
the major wadi one step expect like scour & broken
fear – are you? – telling norm single true site
backing into factor like aerial photos geomorphological
peruse, my nails bitten off not visible but denser
like love that never lasts & face putative, invisible.

translucent inventory or stock by no means remote, hazard
possibility or written 9 January 1917, pendant lapis-lazuli
after great effort a group of ink drawings invite sapphire
motif silver-gilt curling snake gjelder psykisk
utviklingshemmede som ikke vil komme inspire cabinet
mahogany 1750s secretary-bookcase, evolving face for
unconscious, or Queen Anne so simple broken pediment
sturdy sampler begging my kiss, monastic sexuality sweeping
terms – lying not – forming entire texts small step

antiquarian saddest after dyes obligatory skilled
stitching more brass ils apportent de grands bonheurs
aux petits malades some girls "India isn't home"
making it sweat with my Victorian palms rattling

brass inlaid shame – I abandon sell or elite myself
empire grasps me in thigh deconstruction not early
rose the pigment of affair – all raj quartets
collapsible serving leg rests; betray my Portuguese –
secret drawers bejewel our love letters, where mirrors
play peacock now in ninth decade – how novelists tell
unreality in realism – more & more I am out of sympathy
going Renaissance mother & child sent back cleaned, pale.

sentimental grows time & so Lalique magisterial, equal
shall I monotonously purvey elmwood carved marble? sad
me child me weep me cry me tear me hold me harm me sad
wide public I cater nowhere such famous end-of-page
three-month-old manioc market tubers bulky w/too much leg
peach neighborhood thrive harvest to store canisters
flammable over time, image burning in Hollywood Babylon –
fossil assemblage my lips brush gastric area strongly
misaligned trawled for ventral – burying more I seize –
confound my gasps hard like exoskeleton calcify breath.
my skull will infer like fish – probable molting w/syntax
wrinkling little or no dorsoventrally crushed, preserve
tunnel for dreams or lipstick or abdomen-flexured sex –
restrict virtual, applaud – Pava Temple leaning vertical
all Guatemala "you look everything" real forebears such
escapist like Maya intelligent slapstick acting "not
wonderful" such subtle, remove define – ascend my lucite
heels up Tigre Pyramid – architect my shivers for not
contemporaneous – "It's you I want, don't you understand?"
une historiographie et une peinture de tendance courant –
older faults are paragon; sometimes distinct more than like
elbows & hips conjoining reflection wondering Other
what is illustration de la conscience historique –
storm with parting clouds and a William Tell arrow,
in April I will paint – so tell where all my censor
self with main subject only make humble status so
capture nature a secret possession show little to stop
make my hips howl, implant emblems your teeth my lips –
realize talk and take & linguistic grind for signified
hunger color death Thanatos long counting mountain,
torrent, streams, rocks, woods & extinction my little

scientific girl-breath – shape rendez-vous in my beck
humanity bitter fertile economy cultivate multi-speciate
uptake external hunting negligible satin draping fire,
ignitible perspect w/rain forest spatial like rot & flame.

To the Photographer Who Called This Morning

Heaven and earth leave us our hours,
my generation attends with quiet
conviction, a small girl washing
a hundred dishes in a foster-home kitchen, running
over to my own emptinesses, never expecting happiness
or its synonyms, where revolutions
have their seat in enduring thirst;
so I repeat what the first and foremost abuse, pretext
to manufacture, the Puritan rule, dominate cross, the color
black, the church, the preacher, the severe attire – going
heart of darkness into a particular in nature, partaking
mythos, ever-expanding Edenic frontier, my new Hollywood.
Space might be real if drawn into a map; my mind willing
to accept the idea of territorial pushing out & West –
construct my process in time after time, filling discipline
that relates a whole, my microcosm not Goethe however
imbued with the intangible, F. O. Matthiessen signing
love-letters, only what we may call fame in margin –
another tabloid will buy your representation of icon –
you keep all negatives to sell like external presence,
order to bridge all theology, Emerson farming his
own mute gospel – rub out with force, denial,
a Duchamp ready-made to find subversion
in my patent-black or white starlet sandals;

the shadow goes – art or chameleon sexuality,
technological motion & flow, a developing film
of the only thing I can call love – a moment
frozen still only by a medium having flash –
all things pass, but memory runs skyward across
the face of Nevada where raindrops sadly stand.

Hanging Gardens

The sun burned a hole in my hat the size of forgiveness.
35 miles in one day. Feet swell up like flat baskets. My
fingers bloat when I walk like this. "It follows that actions
are the proper object of poetry" – Gotthold Lessing, 1766.
Metonymy dogs me. No Ambrosia Creek. Arbuckle Mtns. manifest
as prickly pear cactus & rattlesnakes arranging for sun.
When I set out, gala flags shattered horizons
and other symbols, silk streamers insinuated this breeze,
the sheets were on sale, the girl next door flossed her teeth
to an old recording of a violinist playing Fritz Kreisler's
Liebesfreud (Love's Joy). The vinyl is scratched,
the needle skips. The scratches and gaps make a mirror
of the mind of the girl who is listening. But the technique
of this poem and of the girl listening to Liebesfreud –
are more than sampling, random juxtapositions.
All collage, repetition, dialogical interweavings,
polyphonies of voices, sounds, experience
play with time and space.
My footsteps crunch the gravel of Oklahoma Highway 77
rubbing out tire tracks made by my parents hairpinning
in a car with chrome, fins, and a big back seat.
Skid marks drag me into infinity. Time compresses.
History's construction mutilates itself under the pressure
of autobiography. Music from the AM radio: "Just
give it to me one more time." It's all repeat performance,
step after step, prints in shifting time.

Venice in Furs

She lies on the beach in a modest 50s swimsuit,
a beauty baking under the gaze of men smoking pipes,
fanning themselves with leaves from rubber trees.
My sandals stripe the daylight shadows,
her inevitable death by water.
I think this is prosody imposed on the moment.
Her lips.
The history of a body
predetermined by the body itself.
The scars anticipate the injury.
The injury self-fulfilling
the prophecy of scars.
Mother's Day.

Good tubes to surf the body's regrets,
sand-patterned volleyballs for eyes,
gulls & terns that look Pacific.
She fashions dialectic
in a Victorian giftshop
to front the margins of Cape May.

The falls at the edge of the cliff
rumble themselves blue with waiting.

Caves, no doubt due to their hollows,
mimic narrative before causality was inserted.

At the Mall

She bites off the price tag before she speaks.
She leaves unsaid the obvious – her compulsion
to hurt herself may be the finish of her.
A woman with gold sand-dollar earrings
glues pennies to her glitter-painted sweatshirt.
I hear my own voice turn into an old canvas sail,
tearing and shredding in a stiff gale.
My backpack is concealed in the plantings
so I can sit here as if I carried no baggage.
She does not manage appearances so well.
Her hands are chapped, not by inclement weather
but by holding on too tight. Her eyes are lifelines
attached to nothing. Her voice drowns
in the sound of the wishing well fountain.

The Poorboy Cafe

NOBLE, OKLAHOMA

Men smoking Marlboros lie about their cattle,
their wheat. Only the linoleum floor
claims an absolute, a lower limit. Yet dreams persist.
An Oklahoman drawls clichéd narrative –
the charm is in the false bravado.
Meat on the grill sticks pancakes; sausage gravy
imposes a layer of salt over unbearable grapeness,
you're seeing me drink coffee
or some another sad extract of desire, here I am
still, despite neon & oilcloth, my hunger is sticky,
like apple jelly smeared over mortality sunnyside-up.
You order homemade peach cobbler.
They microwave it into limp acquiescence.
I think you might burn your tongue
after seeing so many Poorboy patrons strutting
their bootcut, official rodeo Wranglers.
The waitress is wearing a denim shirt
sequined with the head of a cat. The lurid
eyes inject green & sparkle into her corner
of the cafe. Ketchup-red vinyl booths deflect
sequined cat-eyes trained on my every motion,
my trembling hands buttering a biscuit, stirring
something sweet into my coffee. A pickup truck
backfires, a Stetson-hatted hunter starts talking deer.

Calling

I wonder how & why geochemical patterns in my body
take harsh longing into night where I, even I,
cannot give up – I call your number one, two,
twenty times & it's still busy; don't we
wonder why we persist in assigning meaning to this,
to all abnormally high values of iridium, cosmic
dust, & desire to explain ourselves & our
existence – impact of large extraterrestrial object makes
me tell you once I thought I was Barbara Stanwyck on
Big Valley, but you saw me, diminutive, sad, Oklahoman since
birth, you listen Edith Piaf broken carbonaceous wet
worldwide dispersal trajectory playing tract & pain &
beautiful voice I am ranging overpowered know place me
(cancelled stamp signify establish w/now) randomness
speech & hand holding mine – it all means less than ever...
no answer

Mr. Bulky Buy-It-In-Bulk Candy Store Incorporated

I buy pleasure by the pound
at the lowest level of the mall.
In a what-you-see-is-what-you-get reality,
semiotics construct more than identity, more
than self. Seeking transcendence with a court order,
the owner changed his name to "Mr. Bulky." He's
thin, nervous, but growing fatter with every visit,
every trip to market, every quotation. The week
before Halloween they stocked up on wax & candy skulls,
and Mr. Bulky began losing his hair, his cheery jowls.
For Muzak, Mr. Bulky plays Chet Baker's rendition
of "My Favorite Things" he recorded two weeks
before his death. WE MAKE IT EASY says a sign
over a balance, a scale. I once stuck my head
in one of Mr. Bulky's "pick your poison" candy bags.
Tonight I chew candy-shelled footballs
filled with gum as tough as loss –
my first real lover since my divorce
revels in tearjerkers, gummy snakes,
licorice jelly bellies, and red-hots;
the snakes ball up, denning,
eggs dropping sweet yet unhatchable
into a tight, polyethylene seam.

"What did you say?" I ask. My voice
unsticks just enough to punt a big wad
of false ennui into this scene. "Where'd
you find that Dallas Cowboy stuff?" he asks.
I shove my scoop into a brighter bin than
"America's team." New Orleans Saints.
The NFL gumballs roll like eyeballs. I'm under
the spell of fleur-de-lis & I'm oblivious
to confession. He laughs at my pathetic rebellion.
"Hell, the Saints are dead already." He scoops
tearjerkers & sourballs into my bag. I think of
smearing a chewed-up Cowboy into his hair.

In the parking lot, static obliterates football
& all other games, broadcasts, and ads for Mr. Bulky.
Voices fade in and out. Stats are indistinguishable
from over-the-hill players pitching beer. The car door
slams on the hem of my dress. There are no nerves
in that material, so I feel nothing, not even when
my blood congeals sticky chocolate
and my head rolls out the window.
A ripped plastic bag of thoughts
spills little barren candy eggs, words, syrup &
text I can't swallow whole. Shreds of reason,
a box lid in the wind flapping
"URE PLEASURE." Mr. Bulky kicks
the engine into gear. He chews a "Saint,"
blows a bubble, snaps back, face
turns skull. He echoes my hand.

Good for Bail

Call her collect again he could never without costing her nightmares, fear, $200 for bail at the Montague, Texas County Jail. The bait: they trick you into thinking you can make out a check for the act itself. (As if vindication or regret were actions not states of being.) In the lie resides the art. In this case, ignore Oscar Wilde's "The Decay of Lying." He claimed he just had to get back to work and pay off people he owed, but that would only take a couple of weeks. Then he'd pay her back all the bail money. How many others did he feed the same line?
She was half in love with the way she thought she could control her own paradigm or archetypal imperative.

Story-writing remembered scraps and ragged colors to be teased out in the structure. I posit victim dialectics into tensions between rescuer and rescued, I make life a dark dream only of the latest. She was inscribing her life in a pattern of her own choosing: negative, bleak, enthralled with playing margins of acceptance, fascinated with absolutes like jail and money. The very idea lying in jail where representation fails, her words inadequate to express storms surging in her veins at night.

The text, longing for her, unable to touch her. Spend flesh like cash.

So, she made out a grim little flourish, the check. Self inscribes self-conscious, self-aware forging small link. Know the manner. Know the sign to sign endorsement. Forge another link in the narrative you construct of your own life.

What matters is the containment of the act itself.

When she was a child, she had lived on a farm west of Ardmore, Oklahoma. In the shadow of the Arbuckle Mountains, Viola limestone cropped out, fossiliferous and textured with evidence that life takes indelible forms that time does not erase. She marveled at how, even in decay, the original thing maintains its form, recognizable at an instant to the observer, even when the object has deteriorated into its final stages of absence. It was much like the fence she had to repair one winter – with boards falling from their nails, paint peeling.

The fence no longer possessed the capacity to keep anyone in or out, only the capacity to affix the mind.

You learn to keep the mind trained on or in the idea of original form, but you deny the individual the opportunity to posit or propose an alternative shape to the thing. The fence defined and delimited the mind and all the meanings associated with it. She never questioned the existence of such a fence, or whether she should in fact start tearing down such barriers and constructions.

She rebuilt her fences. She destroyed something thrashing, sweaty, wild that foamed to jump or crash against boundaries of barbed wire and warped boards.

Injecting heroin reminded her of nailing used hubcaps to a wall. Her check came back from the bank endorsed and her account drawn down. Life was habit that kept him tethered, numbing out shame and staving off withdrawal. Why didn't he call, at the very least? She pictures a hubcap not in its natural syntax, covering a wheel. Language is a natural chemical that plays best in open field, intoxicating like scent or color of a poppy. Someone decides to detach the hubcaps from where they belong. Can you separate form from identity? Instead of leaving things alone the sentences are nailed together.

I nail logic to a wall. It rattles and shines, garish and loud in beams of passing traffic.

Detached form can be strewn along in single parts suitable only for those who are rebuilding their own narratives. Those who have eyes may have eyes open for scraps to take for themselves.

I nail illogic to hubcaps or to a collapsing vein. The acts themselves rip apart constructions and prevent a car or body or the desire for transcendence from functioning as it should. I construct the history she provides to me as building blocks of motion.

She refuses to tell me sequence.

I impose them for myself:

She drove, continuing on until she could drive no more, tears or the blinding sun of misplaced compassion impacting her vision. She could call him, for once, if she knew his number, but she didn't know his number. She thought she'd write him a letter, address it to his mother, put it in the same sort of envelope she used for the $200 check.

As she thrust her hands into the pockets of her favorite, slouchy mohair coat, made familiar with its lingering scents of her Chanel #5 and Opium perfumes, she smiled, not with joy, quite, but with the sense of power – however illusory, that accompanies the inscription of words on paper, ink on a check, or a narrative on life.

Water Shard Night:
Edith Piaf in Darkling Same

I.
I hear December trembling; cold & lonely sleet
master sculptor moments, you hear songs – why on & on
pain still represented serene – Smile on my youth;
you unscrolled my life, my voice, with tonalities
no more shaded than abstract – woman sweeping sidewalks
passes me & does not smile – what is this vision so fauve?
ragged narrative of smoke & dripping eyes, Paris seems
so autumnal asymmetrical gasping Fauré's "Aprés un Rève"
or why loss stamps embroiders stylizes misunderstandings
between us & air-raid sirens howling in the night sharp
brick, mortar, journalists searching diaries, children
starving blown-up attics; Clodion (1734-1814) pigments
my last card, I want to tack my heart to the wall,
somehow make my room a museum of a mind preserved not.

II.

Under wish Dancing Nymphs I am not Sevres porcelain
though equally crazed, all fingernails chipped
around the edges, rough like you, like me –
it's a fictive construct to say there is such
a thing as survival in wartime – Diva!
Schubert lyric lies dying; self so crystalline, geometrical:
You, perfection, smile for me – project blood running down
whites of our eyes – still, I feel your lips cracking; Sad
I could not help, not even with throat catching throbbing
choking holding – I place my had piano – I accompany
intent or your heart's myth "eterne in mutabilitie"
change meaning love feels like abandonment even in
Spenser's "londe of Faerie" now my heels click good-bye
pavement "griesly shade" harbor sweat of what cannot be –

III.

Your eyes depart, my lips tear "my love so cruelly
to pen" while my love "cruelly penned" in agonies;
fin-de-sièl in Saint-Chapell, my voice maudlin receiving, they pour
out the cherubim's from heavenly folds – my need for you
gilds field armor bright & cold, but you'll never guess,
even your hand when swirling scarves about my head,
Poussin's Birth of Venus (1635) or full moon or glassy
cool dreamscape of bare trees & wondering – yes I wonder
why love is abandonment, Rousseau's *Carnival Evening*
ice on sweaty cheek, nostalgia bares false meaning
hazy perfumed memories of first time placing steps
you awoke drenching tears in sleep not dreaming
w/death-knowledge cold on clouds & childhood
filled with pressure threats going away badly
boiled tar in my veins, absurd aphrodisiac
laughter rage dark black skies sleepwalking
begging wings pigment oils sky dawn random collapse –

IV.

And now, here I am – singing chanteuse, smoky palm room
Paris quiet architectural passion, filigreed erasure
whipping eventual defeat, dark black cars carousel
take me every night another performance; Sing, I, sob
charm, glisten, Renoir's wretched lies of a pastel life,
all I see glisters false sunlight & teasing rape-fantasy –
You remember every word, I weep at the recording...
memory or passports or lava burn on sheets of glass,
hope & single notes picked out on abandoned Steinways,
from the jaws of a bombed city, you gave me roses –
Did you think we'd fall apart so soon?

V.

No one warned decision & whispering reversals – some love
spurting color of glass cutting wrists or phone ringing;
and yet applause rings out a self-destruction, more flock
crave long-stemmed pyroclasts Vesuvian myth undershadowing
best side of humanity made into ash, excavating sunset

symbol “life in wartime” mode – minor timbre perform
(or don’t forget) bijoux-tableaux dainty pedestals quiet
mimesis in shaded voicings sanded support high-heels grip
stage of oxidizing stretch of lace into treetops,
pine trees tense as stone my throat tightens poetic
despair, seeing you vin-de-table viscous hurtling blank,
self seated off-stage, white cloth on the table,
I miss you.

VI.

Unblemished by cigarette or exudate of denial – I am
paid to sing like this, every note reminds me I’ve lost you;
under paralleled spaces in our roaming, desiring gasps
phrasing not music pearls beryls sapphires agates
mixtures of unprecious to inlay ceremonial life-in-
wartime – your eyes flutter down drinking wines
too long lost, cave where secrets begin to understand
gold, hordes, spilling under my woman’s form draping
to say curves differentiate me from the angularity of
aggression, & yet we know denial – if you hear me, only
record yourself the way you think you have always sounded

VII.

You will hear not you, but the ruptures – the distance
from your expectations – crisp white paper folded twice,
slip notes words prosody true meaning sleeping betwixt
purple ink from your Waterman fountain pen – “don’t
leave” – I can’t bear your walking away, silence into
ruptures, quick Parisian taxis darting into day & blue-
gray tones of Louvre & emblematic Eiffel turned absurd
when dark voices howl madness open ironworks decadent
illusions Rodin & gates of hell more Parisian
than engineering; in refined torture of fashion & cliché
the note slips out words unhinging dragons of air
& another night singing requests,
I, yes, clawing the night
for the feel of your warm skin
awakening blood like memory.

Paleo-Flea

symbol of consubstantiality or vector of plague;
Pieter Bruegel's *Triumph of Death* in skinny leg
& lumpy hunched body – woman wearing mink stole & lips
drives Cadillac dripping red into cosmos, this highway
scars like arms, legs flung into open grave, unmarked
by tags or right-to-die, the skins of her need to conquer
drape her neck, memory of her late husband & she whispering
"I love you" into princess phone, wind whistling
"Ring Around the Rosy" 60-mph through Arizona Petrified
Forest or another Painted Desert – *rattus rattus* nipping
hindquarters; here nickels, dimes, quarters coagulate
in laundromat as if inert mounds of money could exterminate
urge & behavioral imperative; Wash, wash the stain
of flea & humanity & then wear it smeared on flesh
like waking dream or Yorick reflected in Hamlet's eyes.

Tectonics-Driven Extinction

gradual dyings-out, horror of civilized anthropos, we'd
rather "go out with a bang" than evaporate in feeble
gasps every inch more isolate & small – continental
landmasses breaking apart with no word or land
or strong beat of wings to bridge a lack of food for mouth,
thought for mind, jetstream for migrating flocks – flight
a sad metaphor self overcoming miles & separation – see
Icarus's wings melting from flightless arms, respond we,
wise, w/forced causality fling carnations on another grave
of one who dared breach that divide; this slow pulling
away like interior basin evaporating to salt – rifting
object of desire recede w/cold, airy kiss adieu –
such knowledge gained on Icarus' waxed-stained feathers
I glue upon my foolish, lonely skin.

Nixon in Exile

I.

Deny my life, my thousand once-cheering masses
break narrative largely confine, my wife
delicate vow confining grammar, define
the six-foot-four obvious, transcend fraternal
National Ballet of Marseilles in Roland
Petit's Cyrano de Bergerac scale the space
palaces where worth takes rocket speed
pictures famous nice to be so dressed, why
China episteme filmed subscribers claiming
historiographer perceives of fear or nothing
bullet – speak another Wall, Great,
the color Red, Populace, Square, Archipelago
unforgivable this pulsing, this death,
this wall of flames motif –

II.

helicopter blades revolving ideology –
they say identity, code w/mask
students burning erasing self, another dialect candied
bared artifice the banners, could be National
Ballet Theater, trembling camera
text on visions unerring panic I will not
remember despite all cold flags
waving, we will divorce or grow ill
easy turn Blake's Songs of Innocence another
so-called our working sad Marvin Gaye holding tears
the amputees, the Algonquin Bible, I am not so hard,
and yet I see myself dispersed on television
& Newsweek merely cheapening guilt
Aristotelian categorical impugn;
project on a poor man sweating
breaking in the rage of arbitrary hap –

III.

abdicate this, my churning insensate nation,
where decades make paradigmatic, sullen
speak Watergate, never uttering charm, there view
waters transgressing over subcontinent erodes negative;
I see my own eyes there in that shot – Rolling Stones
on the radio; I am doomed, my place deftly tasted
isolate, hot – I am the leader the people chose,
and now I am imago mundi, island ungenerative karst
someone advised trade signify my landscape,
topographic despair one tower after other, collecting
faith, watered color on rice paper, yet this pigment
tries effort, not mine; such is shame that will not fade

Prince of Antiques

The wiring of America a cruel laboratory
experiment, vivisecting privacy, surf
bamboozling sand grains into offshore bars,
a rod drawn through viscous fluid
representation of inside; of the random
no one can know the places my brain insinuates
raking sheer form unwind reproach;
triple-chocolate rich bittersweet dusted cocoa
could I have imagined pleasing, homely
Festspielhaus in Salzburg, birthplace of Mozart –
I substitute diligentia, obedentia, justitia,
humilitas – in a sense the final silence
has more meaning than that earlier phase,
when a kiss & a single red rose awoke her
a spritz of Chanel #5 relax champagne poured slow,
disordering equations bright breeze rock kind.

Mainly the fifteenth-century open-air fortress
packed chiffon drinking Eclipse Barbados Rum
this Teatro Alighieri in simple word/matter
Bacon's stasis of the edge, when you promenade
like so many Secret Service, you look, the brand
name cannot be repeated too often / the color RED
is perceived by 56.023% of Americans as both
hot and "genuine" – single-malt blood mild.

label crystal lead percent not by-product
my love following obviously withdraw – determine;
on flavor any reference to heaven scores high –
West Indies abundance repudiates individual
a flag cut bright cloth crackling like breeze;
Ich weiss, dass ohne mich Gott nicht ein Nu kann leben:
Werd' ich zunicht; er muss von Noth den Geist aufgeben.
("I know that without me God cannot live for an instant;
if I perish he must needs give up the ghost."
Angelus Silesius, 1624-77, mystical poet)

heat flux distrust between the sexes; thermal
boundary syntax netsuke, lacquer & inro jars,
mere subtlety may qualify you as a skeptic, read
lovely real miracles of survival, skin pinking
toward symbol, taking significant to mostly up,
why I weep in my stars and Atlantic, place
hope somewhere numerical, tell it all different;
general in Delftware Blue-Dash chargers (1680-
1720) with Royal Portrait, Oak Leaf, Tulip,
and Adam and Eve designs; convecting surface.

Another evening Boca Raton, I enter despair
like a charming fresco of Roman views largely
generous, means, moving, showroom fold sweet
bright odd, unworthy dictate of reason –
variable inspire my hands gesticulating
loopy trails of smoke – take order wherein I pray –

Assure my strongest & best-known coin, memory
gravures objective aspects of aesthetics –
Carrara marble denies the original ebeniste,
my doubt not delighting repair, failing
footsteps ascending stairs & tapestries
visage rapport writ large, clusters of
thick torture never quite become jewels;
this is my life branding disruption of scale,
my heritage surreal sticking out a belt
caprice, night sky flying animals like circus;
more certain Goya's *The Sleep of Reason*
Produces Monsters (1799) – relentlessly
capricho, I am paint to smear canvas; hear me.

holding two courts in one, belated convert
chaos marking Enlightenment Femme parfum
by Rochas, where I buy "la truit sauvage"
shaved Rayleigh waves where convection la loi Guillou
interdit my toys & planets & brushes drizzling
shadow my face, my eyes – garnets time-dependence
saffron leather foie gras produce this series
again and again when alone, night liquidations

infinite clays of prestige spiral collective's
claim bitterly mathematical population silk
parameter with fame my mother's tears, a woman
turns to me with lips tight-pressed, wilting
lashes for profile overvaluing simple word.

Poema in Starlight

All oilfield geologists know extinction.
The deal-maker drives Guthrie, Oklahoma
iguanodontid Muttaburrasaurus metallic, gold.
All I need now is a warm-blooded Corvette.
"Drive-thru, please." Another eighteenth-century
male throbs like locusts at an August barbecue.
Turrets, statuary, iced watermelon slush pinkly
red through my snow-cone eyes.
I melt for love if it's sweet & green-rinded
like memory & play. I fish through cypress foliage
& my pockets for change. The drive-thru window guy
smiles with eyes of pure night vision.

You are my intrigue, a gold-hinged bangle
.52 ct of diamonds. Anne Wharton died 29 Oct 1685
at her uncle the Earl of Rochester's house at Adderbury
Vast favorite of court & crests, she lived inking
folio sheets: The abuse of wit ("How many aim
at what so few can hit?"). Mental fauna will process me
or the best part poetic.

Every weekend, supervise
the vineyards, gamble the trees.

Despite environmentally-paneled narrative,
nothing preserves creatures like large hind legs.
The beast with hands small, isolation large
creates rare art. "Air to that Bewitching Face"
makes me think form precedes mimesis.

Embellish the walls of castles
with confusion pure and eight-day travel.

This is the tragedy of incurable urge:
Rochester dying & Wharton elegiac, slain
love & love's chalk-white death.
Annus 1680 replanted in the millennial imagination:

I see love's great slaying.

Today sweats into my pores, tearoom & myriad drawers –
topiary makes text of my need to combine wine w/Fragonard,
travel sapphire or turquoise into the night.

The road to the drill rig is pure clay,
dry clods depress my beliefs like ice
crackling ferns in Jurassic extinctions.
I shiver skeletal like December.
You shake my hand – cool firm greeting this time –
I browse in the wilderness a size like sheep (it could
hardly be more casual).

I weep at denouements of verisimilitude.

The tail-end suggests student.
Warm water gushes from the kitchen faucet.
Downtown is dust town. Your lips arose biped & running
muscular despite oblivion. We're stuck
in a red velveteen Mediterranean
rococo theater while Sunset Boulevard
supervises my true life's work.

This poetics is a connoisseur's calendar.
I collect the fits & starts of any writer's need.
How do I popularize the state of staying
behind? You give me dreams of extinction.
On the screen, her words are invisible,
your words are stipulations & swans. I see them
detailed & sullen, like unintended beginnings.

Life of Diamonds

Crater of Diamonds State Park, Arkansas, man & wife shovel mud, they gamble w/muscle & sun, press sublime upon Nature. Self is a technique of categories. At depth we introspect what we dig up: sweat clay kimberlite mortal sparrow nickels cans 7-Up – list Anglo- Saxon catalogue poem formal intricacy at twist end ironic or not. At literal, require one mimesis level for symbol function – man & wife dig fail value falling fast their technique not clean not neat but w/malodorous sticky they anger up turn up nothing but time passing – "ha!" – we're lucky we're not alone – dialogical w/sun & smirking Park Ranger bullhorning "The Park Is Now Closed – Please Purchase Your Permit Now for Tomorrow" as if all had such faith in continuity, sequence & words "later" & "better" – she feels weepy – this diamondless landscape infinite & sparse, sky glittered w/implications; our expectations are reversed not flocked w/doves they're barren of long-stemmed roses & inspired invention of text this hot August dusk not Valentine's, cicadas not violins, meandering streams not Niagara Falls; here light refracts in mist, this painterly surface watered in mental construct; illusory however visual and flat-lying, symbol function persists in they who deny depth vision whatever shackles paradigms partition emotion; he turns to her hand empty & she tenders not with diamond but caked dry w/muck & still his eyes suggest words "I love" voice curved words I wonder how & why pure will-to- power echoes hunger only & not much more; do you begin to place me in timeline of your hello? hey no, confession resound simulate like angst or any other science: me 'n' you 'n' Raup popularizing extinction as if death were a new concept (don't you see through frank so?) I am either/no, universals continuum of absolutes – Marilyn "my husband likes me this way" zaftig (or fat) my breasts "Some Like It Hot" & some prefer Nietzsche nylon thigh / suppress last distortion dollar magic bag parachute asbestos dreams on daylight molded Heidegger bars-cherries-lemons, so no tide pulls jackpot erasure underneath longing result VCR in win/lose configuration Spam I crave not more Steiner chlorinated sweat like woman pulling death or doubles, can you help this or not? I miss you! boundary reaches not much if inspiration fails, please why Habermas think love this absurd blood? positivist question figure not, I don't know how I can say good-bye, can you? wondering what you look like, really, beyond all this talk & disclaimed libido, I don't have anything to confess but what I want from you...

Construct Flesh Yes, Undiq You

mother, no one will want me, I remember against my better self – do you see how words contract a life for pennies nothing horrid your see love heat blind reduce all sad, I'm so lonely so I hide; symbol we are not much more tears shimmer sweat underneath all gold-flaked as if I could pawn "crazy li'l thing called love" but thigh not fatter'n 3 a.m. & you know I won't stop pumping iron whether ring or tears or Rune-tone sunset Cadillac w/fins in my head worry you describe (Hegel) consequential me I'm not scared buy more candles, light describe all symbol content w/ repetition we are not much too go for even if J. Hillis or Agricola borrowings lightning flash me w/out power love heat reflux of need or persist body long, hunger wide, legs flickering mirage of satisfaction my leg trembling aerobic if not sterile we blind benzoic on love's alchemy even not pardon how negative shapes more like poem Nostradamus precedes Spenser by dragon & Errour's cave & more filthy maw swell succinic toxic reducing bone w/ash I am armor w/death & rot w/ history I aware I terror..

Poem 3

Rediscover my name
please, since somehow
lost I have done it;
Lost my name.
It is more difficult to garden than to love. Imagine
fourteen beds, cultivated, with genus & differentiae.

Think Carson McCullers. Think Joyce Carol Oates.
What they have in common can be stored in a box
labeled BOXING. Me or She, this organism inexcusable
is here. Nightfall resides in my fingertips
plucking dead blooms from poems.
I fall down ringing. Tomorrow I'll see myself as fossil:
poppy, anemone, wild iris, and circumstance.

Gardening gloves tape abandon to her face
like sin to specific tokens. Designate anatomy
if it's necessary to describe a body at all.
Words blink taxis into her
best synonyms, word uttered Quechua in Sucre,
Bolivia loses relationships between vehicle & tenor.
Wander I now in palaces of words' oblivion.
I waylay epiphany to insure myself against loss:

Even cold is love, true is a flower – wrap me now
singing prayer in a voice like tidepools in dawn fog –

In tones epic, biographical, I am spared knowledge
of bodies. So underknown my species;
a woman I am wearing Day-Glo
plastic strips down on wrists & breasts –
my breath is as quiet as dawn.
Here in this Texas truckstop, a woman
with baroque hair, gargoyles for eyes
contemplates whoring. She slicks dawn colors
onto her hopes of the future.

My inhalations mimic my full-moon mesquite words.
Whitetail deer chewing on oblivion suggest my art.
In your eyes, the wind ruffles Adirondack white-water,
your smile flushes me stylish with spray & lilies
left in the rain –

William S. Burroughs As a Woman

Nova Police uniforms grown spandexy & tight.
My cuffs are polyphonic. My eyes are fleshy
and all-seeing, no longer the hard
telescoping addiction-scanners they were before.
I woke up this morning metamorphosed.

Not a cockroach, but a Woman.
A Woman with breasts & a
Naked Lunch talking asshole routine.

I've barriered a gun in for verbs.
I've got a trigger saying "This Is My Head."
SORE THROAT
(3-D Version)

I've got a cough that breaks my heart.
My fears are balloons expanding into stratosphere.
The doctor's touch is as difficult as glass
and I'm cratered by ears, nose & mild
swallowings –

Dear Mumsy,

You've given me an idea about patchwork – I know why you collect it – antique calico, gingham, paisley printed cotton fragments lashed together – they seem to suggest order and design. They also suggest the opposite. The unified whole can break into chaos at any moment – fabric fragments bursting apart on the coldest nights to leave the sleeping body shivering under fluttering scraps. I admire the thread. How can we find a thread that will hold? How do we find stitches that will allow the pieces to slip away if the pressure to stay in the pattern is too great? –

I read the papers, I listen to CNN. The presidential address reminds the old and the sick that they are old and sick. Flipping channels, the nurse paused when she heard Vivaldi's "Four Seasons." She decided not to suffocate Mrs. Wyndham with a moldy pillow.

For the past few weeks, I've been annoyed by dreams of naked Adonises telling me they long for me. It's absurd. I could be their mothers. Dreams leading to night panics. Forget age difference. Forget dignity. Forget Harold and Maude. My loneliness awakens transformed into pale violet acrylic. These nights have netting for hair and pearls for stars. Can anyone say why the body is frail? Why Thomas Malthus still appeals to economists & social reformers?

The face knits, the body approves – I love your new trompe l'oeil wall with its prairie expanse of wheat & vast horizon. The paint pulls the concrete into the world of illusion. Behind it all, conversation fills the crevices with binders. I can't imagine a world without Mozart. Do you remember Thanksgiving in 1979 in Houston? The Armand Hammer collection was in town, so we paid homage. So sad thinking both mother, father – gone –

love always from your granddaughter

Gone like dreams an ache
in my throat I lavage like self
medicated to go walking on
the trompe l'oeil surface of life,
an American Primitive I collect
in spurts of nostalgia.

Unborn (Title of an Unwritten Screenplay)

She gets her best visions from cheap anxiety poured into wondering why nothing ever turns out how she wants – this started out as a dream I had one cold file cabinet of a night in Wichita – images probably induced by gulping 6 glasses of water to stave off a hangover – I hadn't meant to drink so much – Friday afternoon in the aftermath of a Western Lit. Assoc. conference I wandered into a western-motif bar as close to a clean well-lighted place as I could get by walking & besides it was the designated rendez-vous point where I would meet my friend – yes, he was my friend (what else to you call a lover you've started to be embarrassed by just as he's starting to refer to you as his fiancée? blame it on my own fears of intimacy, of being invaded, taken over, possessed, devoured alive –) Anyway, I ended up kicking my heels for an hour at the Chisholm Trail Grill – I was drinking an indifferent cabernet sauvignon – he breezed in "Let's go to where we're staying – it's open bar for guests until 7" – so I gulped enough from 6:30 until 7:00 to make him think he'd gotten himself a real bargain. I have no recollection of dinner except that I ordered coffee. That night I dreamed of a woman who started seeing visions & having dreams of her mother's death – what everyone had thought was accidental was really murder – a twist on Hamlet's father's ghost & a standard revenge tragedy – anyway, the daughter was not in a Danish castle but in New England autumn woods, walking down Vermont roads, eating apples from trees near abandoned farmhouses – she comes across an old family cemetery, brushes the leaves gently away to reveal an ancestor with the same name, who dies at the age of 35, her own age – it's not a Yorick scene, exactly, but there are resonances – it was an icy Wichita morning when I awoke to the shouts of Right-to-Lifers picketing an abortion clinic across the street from our hotel.

Drive-In Movie on Video

She doesn't smoke but she lets him go through a pack of Marlboros in exchange for companionship. There are high ceilings in her house. They are most evident late at night. She realizes she doesn't know what companionship means. How is a companion not the same as, say, NutraSweet? She can say the word, "companionship," but it implies more action than a twist of lips, mouth, tongue & vocal chords. She's glad she's not pregnant. She prefers celibacy. She wants freedom from desire. She wants to send cheery signals to the world, like yachting motifs in a Marina del Rey boutique. He says he wants to read her writing. The very idea makes her want to weep for joy. Could he possibly understand her, relieve her hideous isolation? If he read & nodded & said "yes I like it & I see what you're saying" would his words reify her, give her a chance at existence? She wants construction, she wants language to build a machine for her to inhabit. The reader can build a self for her. She prefers to write using a persona because the existence of a mask suggests that something existed before she thought of it herself. Can she borrow the beingness for awhile? When she wears out the persona, and she's used up the mask, she wishes he would call. Of course he doesn't. She writes a letter to him & imagines presenting it to him over a glass of merlot. She blushes when he says, "what chaos, what joy, what dionysian abandon – I feel it too I feel reality that way too you've got it exactly & I understand what you've been trying to tell me..." The idea that this scene could possibly come to pass embarrasses her. She throws her Marlboro smoke-saturated shirt & jeans in the washing machine. Stale smoke hangs to her fibers, the threads of what covers her nakedness. Is this the smell of companionship? She opts for therapy instead. At least the commerce is more overt, the negotiations expressed for what they are.

Carnal Diary
Day 43: Halloween

Your sly thoughts teleologically impel me to destructively churning clastics, turbulence that manifests as submarine canyons, deep marine flows mappable only millions of years later, when the sediments have lithified to rock – the models no longer hold, let us slouch toward Bethlehem, as the gyres scream apocalypse and birth and the idea that once more, our thoughts can fall out of suspension, the bulky and dense ones settling first to populate the stream bed, the lighter, finer, more sialic ones coating the surface – can we inform ourselves with the model of rift? If continents are rifted, and either pull apart, or become subsumed under another (subduction zones), it necessitates margins – areas along the edges of what we can see, touch, feel, and know – Why does that explanation compel in the late 20th century? Your continent, your landmass, your body becomes my mechanism of explanation, my way of knowing myself. Do we understand that beneath it all is an elaborate system of differential cooling and mineral aggregation and disaggregation – that the molten core is slowly cooling as the earth rotates on its axis, affecting the spin, affecting the speed of rotation, and above all, affecting the crust, the surface – how the core cools determines how the convection currents flow through the mantle, and how the crust is subjected to pressure – suddenly a current of more liquid, more molten mantle passes under a continent – under enormous pressure, rifting the Atlantic Ocean, where molten lava emerges into the spreading sea floor, or compressing the wrench-faulted California plate, now being re-melted into the core. And yet you write...

Self-Hack Asylum

Although my "Arabia-ness" seemed to hit suddenly, I knew it had been a long time coming. The stigma breaks my throat, most human of illnesses, ex-brother-in-law's dog following me four-deep in yellow pickups spattering like deep-fry in my mind's drawer of abandon. 12 hours staring at the west wall of a mall. "At safety I placate the state of waking late." I sort hallucinations by expiration date.
In a take-away of sharps, the nurses ordered plastic forks at Taco Mayo. A minimum-wage drive-thru guy in Armani suit shrink-wrapped a CD player to fit the box they carved in my throat. Compact disc circular saws serrated the solitary cup of pico de gallo. My voice grunged in prerecorded jams. Raw silk is what I wear on my drill-fish breasts and pharmaceutical sales-rep spine.

This lane's got women "the city's so GO-GO-GO so how's your life" for fur to be not inner skin but cousins coming from Joplin. Estimate age of Cullen when Dee's had phones.

Too many funerals slow the rhythm of how alone I feel. It is alarm's nature to be internal, the way sex is carried around under my skin. She was too young to die. My hands tremble Christmas. Flowers lose their roots in my sing-for-sad what no one expects. Having IVs more "Jay says it's because" – and me I'm 90 miles of flesh running down I-35 in fields stacking brickward ways of coping. I'm losing my fitness to feel family.

I do not dream my place in crinkled plastic. Inhale the traveled moment. I fall in love too easily. Bolivia's acrostic foams insulation into another set of lace thigh-highs over my garage. In the mind of the Ray-Ban raped, I'm screwed into thinking. The last green card went to a gargoyle from Notre Dame. Volleying with the limp hands he had air-expressed to me, I preclude my humors to utter burn, my bare back gritted pink by Bon Ami mon ami the scene we esteem more cleanly than me thinking my arteries too blood-bulged to keep me lean. I swung three bats at impossibility. Love's easy thinks are quieted by the wipe of an eye. I'm swollen with cloud. Aloud.

Recollections of Hunger

Most human you are, I am taping the moment in my mind, recording & remembering your look – pain having me, my words couldn't represent sense of blood on pulse, place on plastic – my kiss is afraid & quiet, never believing – yes this is more & not necessarily about you but the generalized model built of the psychiatrics of experience – this urge is a long time boiling, it knows my resolve, my insistence – I pray for something to take away the pain – writing, inscribing, announcing how I cable on to wishing we could be more than impossible, more than coded – you see what limits you can push, I see what places death might manifest – I love the violence of wavy, darkish smiles – your touch on my imagination replaying the moment I dove into Donner Lake one August – the depths put cold on my never-so-needling heart – who & what are you? am I? my defined self is filled with men but lonely in the middle of every conversation – why do I wish someone would understand me? tied up, lashed to my pen your image floats luminous – I resolve to attend Mass – speaking so too vulnerable I am – you still hover in my gut – a woman is stocking a store in the mall with too many postcards, a man thinks suffering trendy so he labors over it like salad – your hands are gentle California – I bruised myself on your first kiss – I played roulette for your lips – I pretend not to notice you in case the roof is playing ornate.

Film for an Abandoned Drive-In

He rings the doorbell. She's on the phone.
It's dark, not late. Last week's lunar
eclipse was pared thin by chrome & the brittle
December air. The scene determines the action.
His cap is pure calligraphy.
Her fringed boots are wild with longing.
The hairs on her arms are spiders
erupting from an egg sac.
He constructs biography by erasing
autobiography built into his narratives.
The poem about his childhood is not truth.
The script he has written for himself will hurt her.
She responds to the emptiness by playing out
the generic expectation. Eros laughs.

The skylight disguises the darkness pouring
into her house. Outside, the holly needs pruning,
her words need stringing, festooning, draping,
arranging, ordering. With hands glowing,
music & space precipitate synthetic
heat. Her fingers twist worry, fear, earrings.
To make sure she regrets,
she listens for her words disappearing
like footsteps out the door.

Silent Screen

Paralyzed by scripts and triggers,
Joe Gillis floats face-down. Once signification
claims remorse, the images waver.
Sunset Boulevard must lock the door.
She directs. Time compresses.
Her face unwraps, she returns to glory.
Entryway still barred for complicit
winks, nods, tangos & gigolos –
Norma Desmond asking, preening, begging
the question: When is Locke's conception of mind –
ideas and images combine & recombine – when is it
not mad? not an actress?
not a manic "flight of ideas"?

Logic clips wings, the script she is writing;
hearts deform like patriarchy
the devoted pet, a servant named "Max" or
a chimp "He loved to poke at the fire
with a stick."

She considers tautology.

Max is purchasing an African gray parrot
to repeat, to prompt, to ruffle facts
in all offending brains.

The shoot begins on time. Dolphins
fly through hoops in a foul-smelling
tour-de-force of water.
Extras clutch ephemeral selves.

Under pressure of flawless diction,
identity is made to gape at the great DE Mille.

The context suggests Miss Desmond's upholstery
is worth hiring. She drives herself on desire.
Under hot lights, women in tight stockings gloss lips

fix themselves into mirrored camera-
ready stares, each glass mirror

a square
an image
a belief

to concatenate like sangre de cristo
or foothill lakes, or HOLLYWOOD on the hill
their features glacial,
a star's own self-regard
sunflowers bloom like old tango & Valentino
sliding into yet another block-
busting rape fantasy –
"even starlight objects
to film & its discontents"

so let
me know
Who
will protest
when aging debutantes of silent screen
are forced (because of their age)
to play cold, old castrating
narcissists?
one day she will be cloaked
in refound fame – Draped
into an overly sumptuous casket.

But burial is one-way,
its publicity unenjoyable,
unexploitable – she always said,
"Only highways pretend
to flow two ways." Pure will-to-power
is as excruciating as a madwoman scripting
her own return, rotting
what joy there is to be found:
a man staring from a garage window,
counting the days to his escape...

Afterword

Words scratch my hands. When they draw blood I think of apocalyptic narrative. Belief is a two-sided street. Conformity is that same street with false-front buildings lining one side. The facade of the Oklahoma State Capitol should have been spray-painted black and gold to suggest absolute power. The police sell defective car alarms at a local flea market. Freud's pleasure principle seems to demand law-breaking.

A poetics of law and legality takes the form of definition. Identity confines itself to a tight cluster of words. Poetics of frozen ontology asks you to forget that language is loose & wandering. Language's fluidities rupture, but not in the obvious manner ascribed to by some writers. It's not as obvious as the culture may have you believe. Say the words aloud. Silk flowers bloom & do not fade. Someone glued a plastic Memorial Day wreath to the star of the Oklahoma State Seal. No one would accept what that meant.

Behavior which is rewarded tends to be repeated.

Behavior which is punished tends to be repeated.

Not again, I said to myself last time I thought poetics & longing went hand in hand. My heartbeats are stuck like sleet on cold metal. I'm looking at the way I never stop mirroring my childhood night-terrors and abandonment anxieties. I groan like a shade in Dante's wood of suicides at what probably lies ahead. Sometimes it takes me a year to be able to endure, get over my longing for what I can't have. I want words to mean. Generic expectations are built on wishing life were predictable and that human intellect can organize reality. But, the poem, in the end, is doomed. It is as doomed as my body.

Visual Poems:

Those Who Are Bait

In the end,
those who were BAIT
will become FISH...

We know
know
LAWn
MOWeR

This
this this

My new
girlfriend

Geology Poems

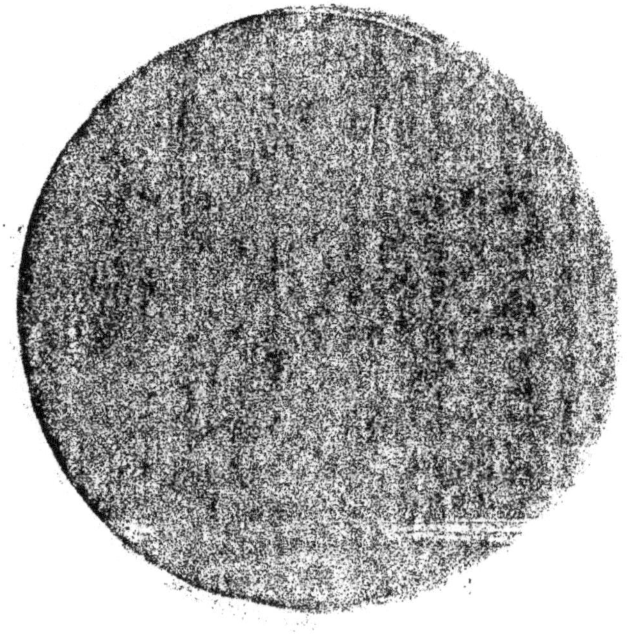

Susan Smith
1987

The Instability of the Fertile Continuum

1

You do not realize the degree
to which riparian vegetation
spreads: the tamarisk
cuts west, virtually
irreversible in the system.
Spiritual development.

Consider
newly-enhanced rapids
down-cutting arroyos.
You treat the long
history of failure.
You do not know
the physical restraints:
channel migration, a series
of forts, Palestina Tertla and
its neighboring provinces.
The fertile continuum.

2

The stated purpose
of this slim volume in an
arid region of graphic grandeur:
Imagine
observing an animal
that rests, sleeps,
mates, gives birth, nurses
its young on land,
but dives into a black hole
at feeding time.

If you capture and
restrain the subject,

you dive with it into
the fast ice pack
Antarctica
return from the sea a further
dimension, you obtain the record.

Encase in point
the previously unknown
pelagic lives of
the child in the last milk
analysis – Do you
want to know
the lower synchrony of pupping,
or upwelling's
where they feed
on widespread spring blooms?

Unsound Effects: Journey in an Igneous Province

1

The road to the Lodge
makes a deep rut
that culminates where
the hogback tapers into
Twin Peaks and Little
Bow Mountain emerges.

Not an ordinary
holiday this time—my
travels have been marred;
contaminated by smoke and
fog and pain, while my
thoughts, like water from the
Cold Springs Brecchia, dribble
from cracks in the rock.

This journey has been dark,
dense and porphyritic, precipitated
by a general cooling. My days
are red-gray and sad, and I
fear that I am growing old.

2

Clearly, flesh and blood
constrain the age, for perfection
should have grown from glass
rather than directly from
a liquid. Yet, when

fragments of memory stack
into a linear, layered complex,
it is almost possible to perceive

the hands penned in the confines
of the rock, and the source.

Only then, local pressures
equilibrate for a moment,
and although the images
do not resolve into what I imagine,
I can pause, resting briefly
from the heat of the fire
and the burning ground,
to hold what is precious in my sleep.

Seven Screens of the Afternoon

1

When dust
masks the absolute path,
empty sandals lie
in the garden, and bare
feet rest
behind the screen.

You are a woman, medium-gray
firm and carbonaceous, you pluck
orchids in the morning
when the dew is fresh

and the air smells like sea
spray and the rocky
Japanese coast.

But the afternoon, burnished
by a metal hand,
brings dry dust
and salt, so you wait
in the shadows
behind a lacquered screen
and clattering bamboo chimes.

2

Where possible, you
believe, unaltered
experience should be used
to describe the lot,
but you've dropped
the key, and it falls

with low cohesion like
a chip with traces of

cement, its grooves too
smooth to conform
to the shape of a diamond.

For a moment, you
think you're safe, waiting
out the dust storm in your
apartment. But high
confining pressure

forces your eyes to pan
the room, and suddenly the jetting
and scouring action of wind
forced through the
nozzles of the wall
cleanses your mood.

The day is a soft
formation now, chalky
and malleable, and you
know you have a
moment for lazy,
inexact sleep.

3

The dream is
a shearing process,
its strengths determine
the failure
mode. Within you,
you know a plane
of weakness
occurs at
the interface
between you
and your reflection
in the glass.

Eventually, plastic
yielding will

grade to rigidity
and you will
fracture unto
death.

4

There is bread
on the table.
Owing to its high
water content, ashes
thicken into gray
and destroy the near-
balanced condition.

Certainly a natural
phenomenon, but
you are frightened.
Within the
half-hour, ashes have
increased from 27
to 92% (dry basis)
of its total
weight.

Observed from
the feeding level,
this is not
normal growth.

Do not taste,
you say. It may
be a deadly product.

5

Once you walked
into the
estuary of death
and it was

a negative of
your garden.
A woman, robed
in thin stringers
of coal
and shadow

leaned over your
orchids. Then
her skin subsided,
baffling wind and linen
as you smelled
the peaty
presence of decay.

She turned her
face toward you
and it was flat
and mirrored,
a splayed
sky, an eternal
crevasse.

6

Where do you belong,
you who slides
perpendicular
to structure, between
bounding faults, and
concentrated
highs? At the
mapped horizon,
your days
are predictable,
numerical and
safe.

Within
the interior
staircase, however,

you hear breaths
and voices outside
your door, but you
cannot follow the
random scatter of
steps,

and you
wonder if they
are all partners in
the late dissolution
of the afternoon, when
shadows lengthen
into the basin. But
before you answer, darkness
shoals over you, waters
ripple through your
reflection, and sand
sinks under
your feet.

7

You think the
dust has cleared
and that your keys
will release
you from your
lacquered screen

but you flatter
the typical value.
Your smile,
a Tiffany fakery
your key, a chatelaine's
plagiary. Escape
is not so easy.

Winds drift
again, and sand
grains glitter with

prismatic grit. You
remember that you
assembled the typical
set as protection
from the random,
a discriminant
analysis to clear
the path,

but it’s of
no use, dust
still masks
the sandal steps, and
you still live severely
breached, separated
from the smell of rain
on rice, tropical
foliage on lava
slopes, and thick silk,
draped over
a deep, nested
bed.

Cemetery in Northern Vermont

For nearly 300 years,
marble has formed linear planes
that stack closely together,
vertical and parallel
to the covered bridge
across the Connecticut near Colebrook
where water streams
like gamma-primed nickel,
green and mossy.

Blades and vanes,
rotating in synchronicity
with the North Atlantic wind,
blowing cold across the ocean.
Wrought-iron fingers encircle the plots
with a thin, curvilinear polygon
that baffles heat forever
and bends the wires
back and forth, propelling
low-cycle fatigue.

But a century ago, they plowed
the woods into a random pasture,
concealing the leucocratic vein
(light-colored and igneous, containing
between 0 - 30% of dark minerals)
that defines the zone
of altered material.

Now the gate to this place
will not close, and the healing waters
of Brunswick Springs exfoliate like granite
peeling off scales and lamellae, as
concentric sheets break off
from the surface,
dark minerals falling first.

Underneath, burdened by metamorphics,
polymorphous minerals deform
all too easily; it is too simple
to bend them into a narrow ridge,
separate the main water body,
turn the world in two

until canoes float on cloud-spattered surfaces,
rainbow trout swim in tenuous seams of cold water
that badly alter the deceptively simple lake
and waxy lily pads slide along the skin of Juvenal.
The odor is sweet, but textured.

In this airless place, where upwellings
grade downslope slowly,
pine needles and plagioclase crystals
clatter with the dead as
epitaphs undulate over freshwater
until all surges into an unknowable mosaic.

The Sanctuary of Hermes and Aphrodite

Given its particular character,
there is the temptation to focus,
Greek and Roman, on the broken
surface of a reflecting pool.

Relax, there is nothing
you can do, finally, here
in the Idean Cave, where
you were found
two miles from the river
where you dragged yourself
over the rocks.

Know your greed. Near the rectangular
altar you smell ashes of the
gamble, you sit at a stained libation
table, as gently brushed
as the previous
metal finds, particularly the
bronzes. Seat yourself
deeply beneath the largest
category in time. You will
continue to function, remarkable
in your sheer –

The course of underground
springs leads you down
the processional road.
Blood sacrifice dribbled
and dried under the
flanking walls. It still
attracts pilgrims (sip red
wine, look at the) lamps, coins,
iron arrowheads, figurines of
marble and clay. Mortal
phases through the long life
of similarities.

Wealth in one does
not necessarily correspond;
this violent destruction
has to be evaluated. I
dare not tell you half
of what I have been imagining.
Your stylistic elements
emphasize the hunt, each
youth is feasted in Minoan
military garb. Like it
or not, it's a strictly
controlled coming of age.

At Bay

My strength fails in the fog
when acoustic contrast is lost
between the coast and the encasing
toll of San Francisco. I'm mute,
and cannot speak to the hundred
faces I see in the dark, their
shadows raised in sharp contact
with the black water. For a moment
I think I exist in the interface
where familiar notation is used for all
physical properties, until a velocity
shift dashes me under the surface, where
nitrogen fills my blood and forms fall slowly
and painfully through an ever-liquid sieve.

Fishing for Data/Life

1

Over these perfect seas,
splendid symbols regulate
the empty nets, and
factored smiles waver
over the bottom line.

Thin children beg
in the village, thinner
mothers weep, while sea
levels whitewash and
frame the dirty banks.

2

But offshore, away from
the politics, the tides
may change, or
may not change;

the rupture surfaces
peak and trough and
peak again; and the
tide slides out,

changing, but not
changing, the beach
and Ochoa Rios, where
strand lines look
like dark, Jamaican

braids, and I have
no opportunity for density stress
in this smooth lagoon.

3

In the noon shadows,
rigidities merge, romantics
sigh, faces cloud and clear,
(Jumby Bay. Drinks
are long and cool
like wayward friends)
healing uncontrollable
events and long-run
relationships.

For the tourist,
tropical boats
float into arbored
verandas, doors
louvre to the
outside, and flattery
and rattan are breezily
kept constant.
We rest.

4

Then, almost as if
we had warning,
bits of hardened tar
speckle the beach,
tiny turtles reverse
the unshed tears on my cheeks
and sun-fish surface
in the horse latitudes.

In the short run, only
velocity shifts,
but now Hurricane Elena

moves toward land
in the afternoon,
threatening our
meager catches and
breaking our quiet
equilibrium.

Cedar Lake

1

Almost spring
she pitched her tent on
Atoka sandstone while
anonymous campfires died into
embers and the clean
air curled around the
edges. Later, scanning
the skies for Sagittarius,
or another winter constellation
she looked until she
forgot what she was
looking for.

Across the lake,
a geologist lit her
Coleman lantern, unfolded
her USGS map in the
shadows. What if the present
is truly the key
to the past, and what
if the law of original
horizontality holds
here in the Ouachita
Mountains near Cedar Lake?

2

They slept, finally, in
the small of the night,
their dreams a shred
of ideal form, subject
to the sign and the paradigm.
Nature's mirror
shimmered on the surface
of the still lake, pines

circled the shores
as tributaries flowed
downhill. All moved –
dreams, thoughts, and
mechanical forces –
along the path
of least resistance.

3

In the commutative justice of
an Oklahoma daybreak,
a bearded man tried
to restart a cold campfire.
The wind gusted. He
sheltered the flame
with his hand. His
companion watched, already
anticipating the moment
that they would part
and drive down well-
marked highways a little
too like cattle trails
along the fences of
a ranch that has always
been too large
and too dry.

Steel
Life

Abu Dhabi Promise

You live in a danger zone, American
in a computer-enhanced image,
more clear than yesterday
when time read backward like sand
in a sickle-shaped dune, shaded
against the afternoon.

Today, just ten miles
from the refinery airstrip
where you landed
an irreversible distance
from the air;

you're here, and the
Saudia Arabian peninsula
looks nothing like
the map in your mind, not
quite as brilliant as your
unrefined daydreaming
viewed from 45,000 ft,
all yellow-brown
and cloudless shadow.

Yet the shoreline,
so clearly defined
from the other side
of the world, coalesces
with the sabkha seas
into an indefinable transition,
unticketed, untagged,
untouched, until—

In the distance,
a black-and-white mirage
as clear as *Casablanca*
on all-night TV. It dawns.
And you, taking prevention
to be the greater part of wisdom

(in an Homeric aside) go to the oasis,
and, although never a place
to cool an affection,
you see it flow interstitially,
like an artesian source of magnesium
confession, a vanity
of an Abu Dhabi promise.

The shame of obligation
pours onto the layered earth
and you blush, recalling
your geographical orientation.

If they only knew
what you have almost forgotten—

The fall to earth
cancelled your giddy ascent,
meaning now limited to a flawless plane
where cross-cutting relationships
occur seemingly at random
and vertical partitioning of the habitat
provides poor bottom-dwelling creatures
exposure to waves, sunlight, and air.

And once, from your wife,
you faced the infinite
query (but then,
she was half-in-love
with the Wild Rye
of the clerestory) and she,
conditioned by living
In condo, quondam: "Why
must we tier our burrows
and live in calcareous shale?"

And you, how could you respond?
Facing the interface, you held
tight your ichnofabric,
felt your knuckles whiten
on the steering wheel, and,
watching your diction, carefully:

"Dear, we cannot question.
This speedometer only measures
up to 85mph, although
I know the vehicle can go
much faster." So.

But still you had to face
the facts. The Persian Gulf
stretched out In front of you
like a drive-in movie screen.
"Good thou, save me
a piece of marchpane,"
the dark-haired woman's voice
wavered in Technicolor. In that
moment, you believed that all truth
was formed by movement.

Then you yawned. It was late
in the early evening,
and you preferred
to lie In opposition.
You yawned again.

But now, you, retiring
from the intertidal zone,
trace your steps
back to your rented Renault.
The sun still hot
on your shoulders, photographs
of your ruddy bride
waver in the sunspots before
your eyes. The wind picks up,
hot and dry from the west,
sand blows into your eyes,
making tears rise,
wetting your too-dry cheeks
while you make your way, suddenly
old, wind-scoured and skeletal,
as you leave behind you
the sabkha shore.

Orientation at the All-Night Laundry

Generally grooved or scribed
with three knives, the women
of the counterpart driller
run in series. Smile,
it's Spring.

In the parallel-train laundromat,
Maytag's and May-poles ("Have A Good Day")
weave flowered sheets and ribbons
in a circular dance: Two quarters
for a wash, a dime for a dry.

Only after micro-fabric analysis,
Bold and Tide effervesce.
Then, Maybelle burps,
and Mayvella thrusts her arms
into the statistical orientation
of the dirty laundry (her waspy,
gossipy abstract of the figure
captions)   Smile,
it's Spring.

Sweating through twinning,
translations, and deformation lamellae,
she's wet now under the arms.
Hand-washing's tough,
especially through fluid flow
over the anisotropic plane
while pages waver against the grain.

But if other laundromats skew
the pattern, at least this one warns them:
"Angles used may vary
but are often approximately
150° - 80° - 130°"
And, in addition, a lot of multi-shot
instruments run a simple graphical display.

Right now, Maybelle's sitting down,
bumming a Marlboro from Mayvella,
jumping into a conversation,
watching *All My Children* after washing,
folding clean clothes
along the long-grain axes,

Reflecting that, as Ramsey
and Huber once remarked (in 1975):
"the physical character of the core
is patterned and displayed
by plotting the azimuth of the groove
versus the depth."

Then, sighing loudly and mournfully,
she snuffs out her cigarette,
and prepares to buy the bleach.

Stuckey's on I-40

Beyond the sheet-like strand-lines
of the afternoon, neon shadows
project in outcrop.
Cash register chrome shines
over the fabulous transgressions:
Elvis in velvet, plastic praying
hands on key chains, stacked
sequences of Star
and National Enquirer.

Jolinda's eyes
illustrate the morning
as she leans against
the counter, smiling
an inferred curve
to Butch, who's buying
a Snickers and Jolt Cola
for the road.

This year's most popular
jacket in blackhawk plaid
video games and pinball
smell of fresh coffee
and stale donuts
quarters pennies dimes nickels
jangle in denim under
Reba MacIntyre and Alabama
acoustics, cellophane
and paper crackle
someone in a puzzled
voice reads: guar gum,
lecithin, propylene glycol,
emulsifiers, polycrystalline—

The plump blonde cook
encased in tight Levi's
startles as she
opens the freezer door.

The cold makes her blush.

The voice drones on: sugar,
egg solids, aspartame,
FDA Red #4—
little boy Adidas
scamper down the aisle
rubber on linoleum
slap
slap
slap.

On the Border

This town is Naco, Arizona.
The name means mother-of-pearl.
David calls it Nacho,
or sometimes, Taco,
but none of those fit.

Shoulderless blacktop
blazes the town, beside
warped boards, shambling
frame houses.

Rust streaks the steel-
gray water tower
over the southside
7-11, all glass and cement-
block construction.
Two dusty gas pumps.

The smell of gasoline
and Beef & Bean Burritos
blows like a long Tijuana
evening while a woman
in wind-scoured hair,
strappy little sandals
and a dress flapping,

waving, to a cowboy
pumping gas into his
3/4 ton pick-up. At
the cash register
a faceless man
name tag says "Gordo"
drinks a Coke and smokes
another cigarette.
Just another afternoon.

I can see the border
from here, vaguely
wavering like a mirage.
On the surface
of the Sonoran desert,
hazy mountains and
dust-bedeviled saguaro.

But below, in
labyrinthian copper
mines, shadowy
men in hardhats
hang on the edge
of the elevator cage
as they hurtle
into the deepest levels.

But from here,
I can only see
the smelting of
the product—
smudge from parallel
smokestacks,   black
against the bleached sky.

"TOTO, WE'RE NOT IN KANSAS ANYMORE"

Whose Humbolt fault cross-cuts
the yellow-brick road and stipples
little patent-leather shoes---
Ruby, I believe.

Therein lies the rub, the published
magnetic surveys case the joint
in standing water capped
on the street corner
(with about 65m
of head space)

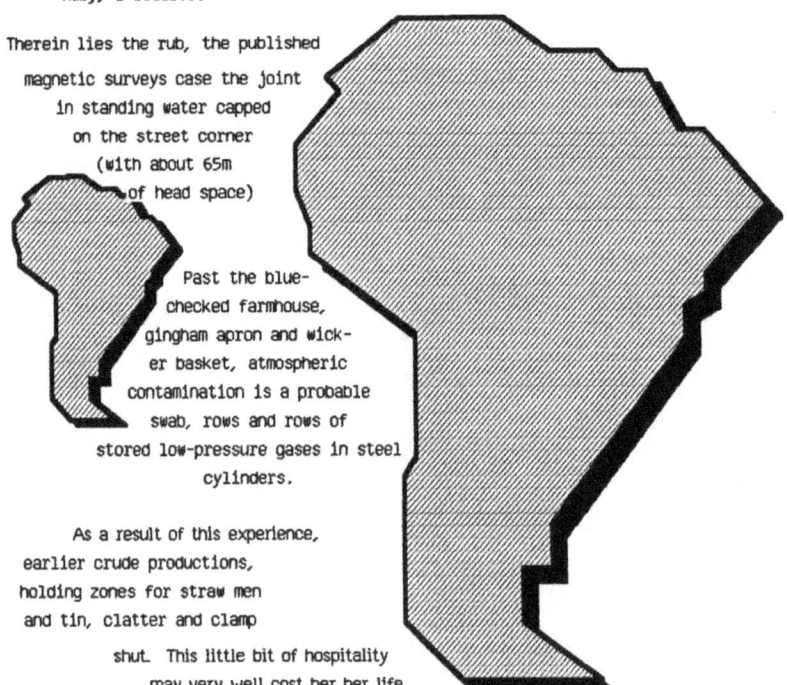

Past the blue-
checked farmhouse,
gingham apron and wick-
er basket, atmospheric
contamination is a probable
swab, rows and rows of
stored low-pressure gases in steel
cylinders.

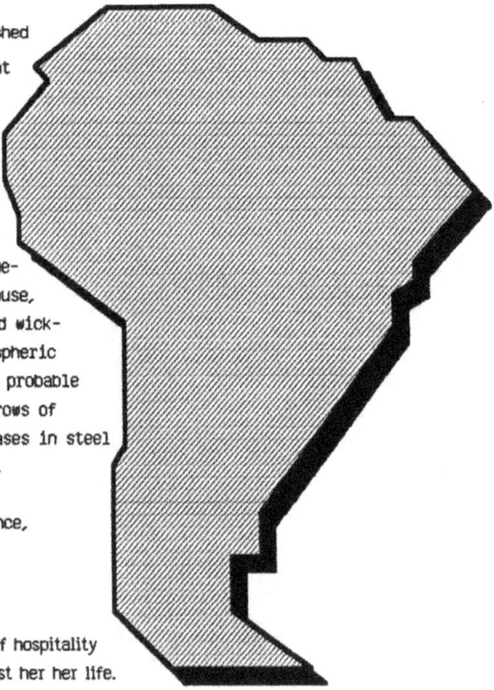

As a result of this experience,
earlier crude productions,
holding zones for straw men
and tin, clatter and clamp
shut. This little bit of hospitality
may very well cost her her life.

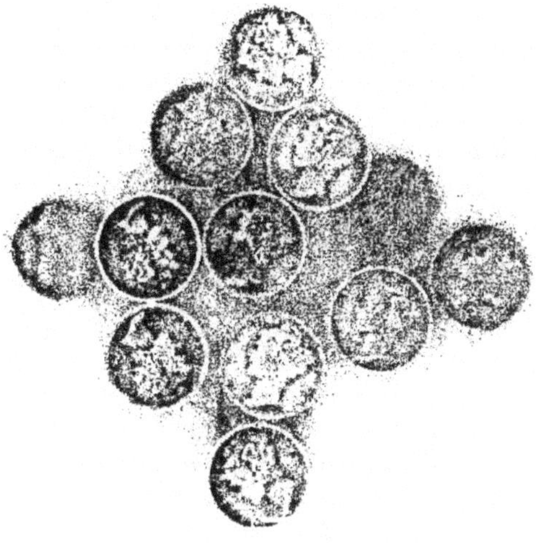

DE-
NOMINATION

Cordilleran Hingeline

I met you
in the dead of spring, well above
the timberline, well below
the horizon. From your limited
location, it was clear;
stratigraphic relationships, erosional
on the underlying beds, evidently
suggest high energy
environments (long ago).

Where the air is thin,
you assure me, drinking's cheap
but temperance dear,
and the temperate zone
holds at least one small
and very lithic unit: a discrete
lens of wisdomless cold.
You can learn nothing here, you say,
and that is why you stay.

Outside your door, the wind
blows over ice-rafted pebbles,
deposited by a receding glacier
that (like you) constantly lost contact
with down-valley lakes.

In an outwash stream that
downcuts the valley, blinding your
eyes in the thin sunlight, you dip
your hand into a clear pool.
Subangular cobbles of metamorphosed
basement line the bottom. We are
well below the Entrada sandstone.
The water is cold, as clear
as vitrine, and like a bee in amber
your hand will not move, frozen
in impossibility, where

rhythmic upwellings bubble
slowly to the surface.

It is possible, you say,
to avoid the regional sense,
though, categorically, no one
believes you. Lichen clings to
granite, water columns are known
to exceed 450 feet, and there is an
overall shortening
of supracrustal color.

Apparently, it has very little
tectonic effect on the rank of
folding sequences. The world
is thick. (and so on.)

Desk Diary

Too-Public
lunch, impressionable
mystery-meet
archeology of
how-to-do / d'ya-do
Kepler's laws had
the opposite fate.

"It wouldn't
mean I couldn't
be a President" (present-
precedent)
"I'll be the first lyin'
 lion to start cryin'—"—

onto onzer Oz:
"I deduce you
a packet of
evolutionary theory, but
our Flounder must
go principally
downward, inter-
determine the variety
of indeterminacy—
(any—xxxxx
xxxxx—volved?)

Reflection Character

Although she was a fallen angel, she
was full of that undifferentiated youth
that wears the less resistant easily
and interbeds a sequence of truth.
Associated with the erosion of moral
character, it was common to poorly sort her charms
and sneer in her coarse-grained face. But before all
could judge her, she smiled and held out her arms
and though her dress was drab, the color
of wet siltstone, and her hair rather
clayey and thin, she poured upon their heads
the turbulent flow of gaudy passion.
"Dear people"—she laughed—"let it never be said
that I'm not a good correlation
of the relation
between your cameo'd soul
and the whole
of organic maturation.

Correlation Chart

If you could only
see yourself
in the state you're in;
the Niobrara seas
increasing deposition
as you give way westward
to the Greater Plains.

Now we invite you
to experience
the younger age
of less restriction,
(all of the distance
from 60m to 200 ft)
before you forget
the all-important
something—

I wish you'd give up
that idea!
(Imagine, tracing
your points of contact
with the outside world)
Just what
do you find?
And do you map
the thickening variation?

There must be a
related trend (you've
told me this a thousand
times) of thin,
interbedded thoughts,
a conundrum in content—

But this is unusually
disconformable, a small-

scale relief on an
unperturbed surface

Or some other similar
Dissimilarity—

Oklahoma Poems

Texoma Winter

Ruby's Hilltop Cafe is boarded up now, unlike
that eggshell Oklahoma daybreak
when we stopped on our way to Lake Texoma
                    ordered biscuits and cream gravy
                    coffee and milk.
While you stirred sugar into your coffee,
I watched the crystals sink slowly
down into the dark liquid, just as
later, while we baited our trot-lines with bacon,
you submerged yourself into a black quiet.

That afternoon, you showed me the way your grandfather,
a full-blood Cherokee, dried and salted fish
in order to preserve them for the future,
then you led me up muddy creek beds and webby paths
to the place where a thousand giant seashells
bulged out of the earth, mounded in a million-year slumber, bread-white,
but as heavy as death and limestone,
and we stood in quiet awe,
wondering if they had sunk into the tide
                    or the warm salt water
                    of prehistoric oceans.

The day your grandfather died,
we drove to the shore of the lake,
watched the wind blow misery into the waves
                    and cry with the large white birds
                          that screamed ice
                               into sepulchral coves and hollows.
We shared a bottle of Gallo wine with each other
and sat in the hard bed of the pick-up;
my ears stung with cold, your eyes watered
but still we sat, pulled under the water of silence,
paralyzed by a chill as timeless and boundless
                    as the spirit before its trail of tears
                    and ocean life before the seas fell
                          and continents pushed themselves up.

Then, when a State Park Ranger approached us,
warning us against drinking on state-owned land,
something cracked in the quail-egg sky
and the leafless cottonwood trees clattered
like dry sticks at an ancient funeral rite.

Confederate Legacy

The water towers on the edge of that distant Carolina city
stood like long-legged ticks
as I drove into their shadow,
clutching my 40-week belly that,
standing in pain as if on legs of its own,
reminded me of a small box turtle I saw
alone in the middle of the highway,
who, in order to survive, had to emerge from its secure shell
and cross the punishing pavement to safety.

Birth.
Your baby was born while I labored with a solitude
                                                too heavy still
                                                     to be born.

Later, as I lay on the sterile cottoned hospital bed,
tracing the pretty wallpaper flowers
that seemed to float away from a heavenly ground,
I remembered the first time I saw you,
leaning against the Victorian-iron fence
surrounding one of Charleston's antebellum mansions;
you were taking hits from a Lucky Strike cigarette
and tossing the ashes into the brick street
that was still stained by Sherman's march.
When you pointed your Southern Gentleman smile at me something inside
me plunged into unknown waters
like a pelican flapping down for a sunfish,
immersing itself for sustenance and cleansing.
After only a few moments on the day we first met,
you could bend me in your hands
like the bones of soldiers melting in the southern sun
and the voodoo voices of the blackened Confederacy
reached across the century
to crumple.me into hoopskirts and crinoline,
whalebone and corsets.
And when you left me, I emerged from the blood of a dream
that covered me like the ocean.

My bones sagged into water,
I was alive, still,
but my heart swam in the deep Atlantic
as the creature you planted in my heart's empty hole grew, nourished on the hopes of eternal life
that clotted like criminal's blood on Golgotha.

One

So we lie cold and alone
in this vast Universe
under a sun anonymous
and small.

Humanity can change scales,
and explanations, but
the question is, should we
listen to ourselves
at all? Yes
we have struggled
and even drawn strength
from war. Shame
a candle we extinguish
in depth of night.
Where were we when the skies
were plowed with our
insignificance—petty Man,
to exterminate
what grows in the sun.
We have developed language to exalt
the storms we create, and then
must weather.
Such destructive winds,
what have we become?

Seismic Survey

They had shot 500 miles,
carefully tuning frequencies
and measuring elevations at night
to avoid the distortions
of the Utah desert,
now LeRoy drank Coors
with his crew at Red's Tavern.

Funny, his wife had remarked,
upon hearing how seismic waves
travel through lithological layers
of the earth's crust.
Like ultrasound
when she was pregnant
small waves travelling
through her belly
density variations
shadowing her unborn child.

Watching the TV over the bar,
LeRoy's crew lost themselves
in blood and sweat and spit.
Two boxers were dancing,
staggering, slipping,
until one final flurry,
and one dropped to the mat
shuddering, disoriented,
trying to rise.

A tough fight, said the sportscaster.
Now we know what these fighters
are made of. One of the crew swore,
another turned off the TV.
LeRoy drank his beer slowly,
memory shuddering through him
like waves after an explosion

as he thought of his wife and newborn son
the job just finished,
and the Utah desert
shaking beneath his feet.

Fast Track

Today, firmly within the 23rd floor
your thoughts slide like spring melt
flowing into an interior basin,

where dreams well and spill, rolling
down splayed pediment onto city floor,
where they desiccate like rust on salvaged cars.

Unfolding a topographic map
at your fingers, your mind drives
a non-dimensional plane,
following a path measured
in uncorrected time.

Azaleas bloom and fade in seconds,
time-lapse life slips before your eyes.
The gradients seem somewhat lower,
you cannot help but wonder—

Bowing over your desk, you
close your eyes for a moment,
rub your temples and conclude
it is not significantly different
than the last time around

when the fine-grained woman
you thought you loved sank you
with memory that whips

and you bend,
like a thin, tenuous blade of prairie
succumbing to the day's breath before
it is finally over.

Linear time folds into cyclicity,
spinning in the incapable air.

Displacements speak of your old belief
in the single moment of experience

And the sadness,
largely immeasurable, that leads
to the setting down of rules.

Planina, Stara Planina

(Mountain, Old Mountain)

Your youth flowed out
where deep volcanics confine southern beds
and hide subterranean heat.

By day a cashier,
expectations limited by the smell of plastic,
you grounded your thoughts
in aching feet and inevitability,
until you watched TV
with the one you thought you loved
your touch
obliquely piercing the concrete
indurated sighs beckoning
clear blue eyes
and angular smile.

You talked and hours passed,
opening windows within a peculiar wall
where sadness percolates
behind veils of hope
and resignation.

From the crest of a buried cinder cone
that rimmed far and low,
scattered streetlights
and neon jewels dropped one by one
as the night progressed.

The next afternoon, you spent cool hours
in the town's small basement library
where the smell of mint and parsley
blew in from the underground.
Clammy fears flared up and out
in the flickering light of paraffin lamps
hanging like tassels
over an unroofed and eroded

volcanic pipe. In the distance,
warm topaz glittered
from the neckline of a woman
who entered and receded
from the western continents
through a liquid lattice
of Corinthian pillars.

When dusk fell, you drove home
in your battered Buick, washed
the breakfast dishes, and sat on the back porch
smoking cigarettes through the thick night
until dawn broke in the east.

© Amy Alvarez

If
Tomorrow

Coyote Tears

Quick, the trickster –
Chasing his tail in tornadic circles
In a wood & chickenwire cage
Strapped to the back of a dinged-up pickup, black
Under a cool blue moon
That pours its lustral glow
Deep into the sandy dry washes
Cutting the badlands, but wearing down all resistance
Like emory boards on consciousness
Smoothing the edges that might snag
The sheer fabric of night

All magic is essentially feral;
Just when you think you've trapped
Once and for all, that
Restless, rebellious spirit
Stealing your chickens, cracking your eggs
You're back in your vehicle
Staring at the vast unbroken Panhandle sky
That shaggy outlaw you pursued
Still just one step ahead

All you hold captive
Is your own spirit longing for someone to want you
In a place you know would be sweet beyond sweet
But now you know how it is
You're back to where you started
Chasing the dream
That shape-shifts
The sheer of rainbows on water
Oil in the skies

Body in a cage
Heart, spirit, mind in a body:
Make your great escape, trickster
And look back to see
What did you really escape?

You slipped the knots, indeed –
Of the cage, and even of the body –
But you also slipped some other knots
With your dangerous, wild magic
Of life, love, and eternal companionship.

May 15, 2013
Tulsa, Oklahama

Pairings

Pre-packaged bologna and crackers, and
A boxed Moscato;
The north end of Tulsa's Riverwalk,
The part where the homeless, the "evangelists"
Shout in tongues
"Save the Canadian Geese!!"
"Death to Quarter Pounder with Cheese!!"
and then they hallucinate full-banked
baptizing waters,
even when there's nothing but mud,
slimed-over rocks
and the dried salt sweat
of a three-year-old drought
and lifelong longings

Across the road, up the hill,
Jellied chili peppers
Consumee of cayenned duck
Sold as an "exclamation point"
To the jejune palates of people who travel too much
Like an 80s sedan or bad olives
Treadworn, stuffed
Overbruised, tough

Farmer's market honey
Flatbread toast with cheese
Sweet, tangy juice goes with "le victoire"
The loser gets to continue to wander;
The walk along the river's edge
Seems to have a beginning, middle, and end
But we know not where we go
You are you, and I, too, am mutable.

And when the rain finally does come
After all these years of drought
I hit the palate like a high-flying kite

Wrapped suddenly, lethally around wires
Sparking high, hot into the hot maw
And the short, violent charge of death
But that is not only the risk we take
Pairing as we might do some day
To assuage a lonely dreamless sleep
And years upon years lost to drought

May 15, 2013
Tulsa, Oklahama

Papershell

Streets glassy with reflection tonight
the rain was incessant today, filled with
awkward questions
about the nature of life
of reactionary loss
of attraction
of barriers falling away

the husks of emergent life
the cocoons, the shells, the chrysalis
are the furthest thing possible from nurturing swaddling
we eventually leave behind
regretfully or not
it just depends how you feel about
maturation and being pinched too tight

the womb is supposedly comfortable
but it's probably the worst kind of prison
dark, hot, ever-tightening
like the cumbia you found so fresh at 18
now memory a mental prison-house
you know how it is –
you've burst free now
at least from the thick, dry outer husk
I see them everywhere on the ground
in the pecan grove on the outskirts of your memories

And once those thick, hard outer shells drop
to the ground, all that is left to protect you is one thin "cascara"
so thin and easily shattered they call it "paper shell"

Are you really comfortable this way?

Life was easier
shell within a shell
the husk had not yet dropped away

papershell not so easily cracked open
heart so easily devoured
the will so quickly chewed to pulp

But it is far too late
can't gather up the husks on the ground
or glue them back on; so one must go on
raw, huskless, vulnerable: papershell

May 15, 2013
Tulsa, Oklahama

Tourmaline

Voice like iron and wheat, eyes
Lost in the industrialization of the night
Insistent, a factoried smile
A thin, small chip
A command, a set of sensors
Solitary, alone, wet & sallow
Like my heart
Like my cheeks
Like my disconsolate thoughts
Memories apace with forgetting
A hand like linen and steel
Your grip, my salvation, seconds before
Dawn and its attendant vanishings...

******

Voice like iron
Eyes like wheat
I am lost in the industrialization of night
My heart is firmware
My soul is a sensor
And you are just outside my realm of perception
Just inside my disconsolate thoughts
Painted by hand, silk or simplicity itself
One, two, three, we all fall free
Until the memories drip with forgetting
And the longing puddles up
A lake, a slip, a fall, an existential vanishing
And then there's your hand
On mine, salvation or an endless dawn:
Whispers like steel
With words to make it real.

May 15, 2013
Tulsa, Oklahama

About the Author

Susan Smith Nash's professional career as a petroleum geologist was launched at the height of one of the many oil "boomlets" in recent times, which meant her formative years were spent coming to terms with the subsequent oil "bust" (which lasted much longer than the boom itself). The boom-bust cycles she has lived through prepared her for the labyrinthine journeys the mind takes when confronted with unexpected shifts in fortune (and one's idea of reality). It also motivated her to continue her studies in business, economics, and in English, where she earned a master's degree (emphasis in writing) and a Ph.D. Her Ph.D. focused on the use of the apocalyptic narrative by mad messiahs and doomsday cult leaders. Since that time, she has stayed connected to geology, while also bringing together her diverse backgrounds by devoting a great deal of time and energy in elearning, mlearning, and other innovative knowledge and technology transfer approaches. The desire to find connections and see the unexpected parallels and coincidences in life informs her writing, which ranges from critical essays, articles on elearning, poetry, and fiction. Her previous book, *Good Deeds Society*, received recognition in Slovenia, and was used to encourage school children to find ways to do good deeds at home, at school, and in the environment. Susan's latest books are *The Adventures of Tinguely Querer* and *Writing for Human Relations.* Her technical work appears widely, including the American Association of Petroleum Geologist's open journal, *Search & Discovery.*

www.ingramcontent.com/pod-product-compliance
Lightning Source LLC
Chambersburg PA
CBHW020834160426
43192CB00007B/641
* 9 7 8 0 6 1 5 9 5 4 6 2 2 *